The Whole Village: SCHOOL • HOME

We want to offer you the opportunity to share ideas with other professiona
partnerships. If you would like to be part of a network committed to buildi..
and mail this postpaid card.

Yes! I want to be part of the DC Heath School • Home • Community Partnership Network.

Date _____

Name _____

Position _____

School _____

Address _____

City _____ State _____ Zip _____

County _____ District _____

Program(s) now used for School • Home • Community Partnerships

_____

_____

_____

Our district/school has purchased *The Whole Village* **Program(s) I've checked below:**

❐ Families and Schools: ❐ Helping Your Child
   Powerful Partners

❐ The Quality Education Project   ❐ The Family Literacy Connection

❐ Principal for a Day   ❐ Education Today

Our district/school is interested in implementing family involvement programs in these areas:

❐ Home Literacy   ❐ Business Community Support

❐ School-Home Communication   ❐ Staff Development

The best place/time to reach me:

❐ School: Time _____ Phone (____)_____

❐ Home: Time _____ Phone (____)_____

DCH/1094/FSPP

Families and Schools: POWERFUL PARTNERS

My district/school is committed to family involvement.

❐ My district/school has purchased *Families and Schools: Powerful Partners*.

❐ My district/school has not purchased *Families and Schools Powerful Partners*, but I am interested in knowing about it.

❐ I want to join the Citizens Education Center network of schools that have made family involvement a high priority. Please send me information about the *Families and Schools: Powerful Partners Network*.

❐ I want to know more about Citizens Education Center consultation and training services for *Families and Schools: Powerful Partners*. Please send me your Publications & Services brochure.

❐ I want to know more about Citizens Education Center activities and membership opportunities. Please send me your Membership brochure.

Date _____

Name _____

Position _____

School _____

Address _____

City _____ State _____ Zip _____

County _____

District _____

The best place/time to reach me:

❐ School: Time _____ Phone (____)_____

❐ Home: Time _____ Phone (____)_____

DCH/1094/FSPP

BUSINESS REPLY MAIL
FIRST CLASS   PERMIT NO 6332   LEXINGTON MA

POSTAGE WILL BE PAID BY ADDRESSEE

DC HEATH AND COMPANY
DEPARTMENT 6252
125 SPRING ST
LEXINGTON MA 02173-9911

PLACE
STAMP
HERE

CITIZENS EDUCATION CENTER
310 First Avenue South
Suite 330
Seattle WA 98104

FAMILIES AND SCHOOLS

Powerful Partners

A COMPREHENSIVE GUIDE

Building Relationships to Support Children's Learning

BY

JACQUE L. SHAYNE

Acknowledgments

A *Comprehensive Guide* is the result of several years of collaboration between current and former Citizens Education Center staff and board members, teams of parents, teachers, and administrators throughout Washington State, and the many foundations, corporations, and individuals who believe that schools and families should be encouraged to forge "powerful partnerships." Their support is gratefully acknowledged.

Citizens Education Center received support from the Washington State Office of the Superintendent of Public Instruction in the form of grants to enhance program development; multiple-year funding from the Meyer Memorial Trust, and funds from ARCO Foundation, US WEST, and The Safeco Corporation.

The insights and assistance of Kendra Fitzpatrick and Joe Pierce were vital to the conceptualization and completion of *A Comprehensive Guide*. Nick Bowen provided essential office and technical support.
Judith H. McBroom is Executive Director at
Citizens Education Center.

Dr. Beverly McConnell provided invaluable research data and insights that led to program changes and improvements and, together with feedback from school teams, resulted in the *Families and Schools: Powerful Partners* model.

The commitment, hard work, and dedication of the principals, teachers, and parents from all the school teams who participated between 1986 and 1994 led the way for program improvement and development. They are the pioneers and the experts who forged strong school-home-community partnerships in many Washington State schools.

The Whole Village: School•Home•Community Partnerships

Program Development Lois H. Tatarian
Design and Electronic Production Susan Geer Design
Illustration Daniel Derdula
Production Coordinator Mark Tricca

A COMPREHENSIVE GUIDE

INTRODUCTION

Home-school partnership is no longer a luxury. There is an urgent need for schools to find ways to support the success of all our children. One element that we know contributes to more successful children and more successful schools across all populations is parent involvement in children's education. *

I f we believe the compelling research supporting parent involvement, if all children are to succeed in school, we must recognize the need for schools to inform and empower parents—to remove the barriers to participation and to assist all families in becoming active partners in the educational process. Rising to the challenge, schools in increasing numbers are working collaboratively with families and community members to create a powerful context in which children and the adults who nurture them can grow and thrive. By listening to and learning from each other, parents, teachers, principals, and concerned citizens can ensure that all children succeed in school and lead productive lives.

Citizens Education Center (CEC), a Washington State nonprofit organization, created *Families and Schools: Powerful Partners* to help schools realize the vision of every child being successful in school. The CEC mission is based on the philosophy that the challenges facing our schools today can be met only by the coordinated efforts of all stakeholders. Parents, teachers, principals, businesses, social and health service providers, community groups, and concerned citizens all have significant roles in assuring all children the highest quality education.

Schools that have made the commitment to family involvement through *Families and Schools: Powerful Partners* report a positive impact on the school system and the entire community. Teachers and parents describe significantly improved school, family, and community relations. Community and business representatives demonstrate greater understanding of school programs and needs by participating more actively in accomplishing school and district goals. Most importantly, all those involved have witnessed the improvement in children's motivation to learn and succeed in school.

CEC believes that the team approach of the *Families and Schools* model is the most effective way to coordinate and expand the resources of a school, its district, and the community for the benefit of all children and their learning. The *Families and Schools* program reaches parents and guardians who think their lives are too crowded to be involved in the school; who have found only failure in the educational system as they knew it; who do not communicate with the school; who believe the "experts" have all the answers; who perceive the school atmosphere as unwelcoming; or whose children are academically challenged or considered at risk. The *Families and Schools* strategies for effective communication enable schools to build, improve, and sustain relationships with *all* families and especially to empower at-risk families for whom the school-home partnership is crucial.

*Susan M. Swap, *Developing Home-School Partnerships: From Concepts to Practice*, Teachers College Press, 1993.

To extend access to the *Families and Schools* model nationally, program components have been organized and delivered in a complete, self-sustaining system for implementation without formal training. The two program components—*A Comprehensive Guide* and *Workshops for Families and Educators*—enable schools and teams to use their resources to increase and enhance family support for all children. With this program, schools can assess their current outreach efforts to families, learn about the needs of their student and family populations, identify school, district, and community resources, and increase their knowledge and skills to coordinate and implement a parent involvement program or to improve and build upon existing school-home relationships. *A Comprehensive Guide* is the handbook or reference to the program. The *Guide* is used to familiarize school staff and administrators with the program goals and the understandings important to implementation and long-term success; to provide the framework to establish a school team and create a school and district-wide support system; and to provide the resources and tools for effective management and evaluation. It is recommended that schools use the process and the guidelines described in Chapters Two, Three, Four, and Five and adapt the strategies integrated throughout the *Guide* to the specific needs of their student and family populations. Additional references and support materials are contained in *Resources* at the end of this *Guide*.

Workshops for Families and Educators is the source for the ideas, guidelines, and materials to create and conduct the activities and workshops. The approach and design of the workshops and activities, which can be adapted for any population, are friendly and inviting and responsive to families new to the school as well as to families already actively participating in their children's education. The *Home-Learning Activities* and parent information materials are also reproducible to send home with families. As school teams experience the program, facilitators and parents will have ideas for activities and workshops and will add them to what is already provided to create an individualized school program.

Citizens Education Center was founded in 1979 in response to the critical need for funding for public education through state law. Citizen activists organized to change school finance policies and continued their work through a Board of Trustees and Advisors. Today, CEC provides the leadership to improve education and community involvement through its parent-school partnership program. CEC advocates for positive educational change, communicates the best of what is happening in schools today, forges partnerships between schools, families, and communities, and develops innovative programs and products that create opportunities for families and community members to be effective partners in education. In furthering this commitment, CEC offers comprehensive support, training, and technical assistance. *

The Barbara Bush Foundation for Family Literacy, the Education Commission of the States, and the U.S. Department of Health and Human Services honored the project for its exemplary work in the Washington communities of Wapato, Toppenish, and Seattle. The project was also recognized by the Surgeon General as a successful national model for building trust and collaboration between parents, communities, and schools.

* A *Business Reply Card* is included in this **Guide** to facilitate the partnership of **Families and Schools** users with Citizens Education Center.

OVERVIEW

▷ **HISTORY AND VALIDATION**

▷ **PHILOSOPHY AND GOALS**

▷ **EXPERIENCES AND INSIGHTS**

The *Families and Schools: Powerful Partners* program is based on Citizens Education Center's successful Parent Leadership Training Project established in 1986 and the experiences of school staff and parents in more than forty schools in districts throughout Washington State in the years 1986 through 1993.

At its inception, the primary focus of the project was to reduce the alarmingly high dropout rate among Hispanic children who attended school in eastern Washington State. Most of these children were in migrant families who worked in the agricultural industry. Initiated in the Yakima Valley of Washington as a cooperative project with the Washington State Migrant Council, the program was designed to provide parents with information about the public school system and to help parents further their children's education at home. Workshops to improve access to formal education and to reduce the failure and dropout rates were conducted by CEC staff at Migrant Council Preschool Centers. For three years, workshops for families were scheduled around the seasonal farming cycle. Volunteers and paid consultants planned and conducted parent meetings in Spanish and English. The program demonstrated that migrant parents were very concerned about their children's education and would attend school meetings, especially if they were conducted in Spanish. However, operating outside the school system, the program had little effect in changing school practices that would allow parents greater involvement in their children's education.

The results of the project indicated that poor communication between parents and educators impeded the establishment of school-home relationships. It was evident that workshops needed to be presented at public school sites by school staff to facilitate the transition of migrant children and families into public schools. Citizens Education Center published its first parent training manual— a series of workshops for parents—to help parents and guardians understand and participate in the school system and the educational process. Eventually the parent workshops were opened to the entire community. As the reputation of the project grew, so did the number of requests from *all* families in the community to participate in the parent training workshops.

The second phase of the project was a "replication phase." CEC offered to train teams in public schools to implement the workshop series. The former consultant model was transformed into a "training of trainers" format. Rather than training parents directly, CEC staff worked with a school team and parents who then became trainers of other parents. The purpose was to encourage schools to bring educators and parents together to talk about their children's needs and ways to encourage their development. The response was overwhelming with more schools applying for the workshops than could be accommodated. Educators were convinced that parents needed to be involved if schools were to achieve their educational goals for all children. The program became a vehicle for many kinds of opportunities for schools and families to interact.

The replication phase of the project was notably more successful than the first phase. CEC required each team to include a principal, thereby guaranteeing a degree of administrative support. The team also included teachers and a member of the community. In this phase, it became clear that team burnout would occur unless the responsibility to carry out the program included more school staff. The team structure itself helped to sustain the effort because all team members added support and enthusiasm and shared the responsibility. New workshops and materials and resource information were added to focus on diverse families.

By the third year of the replication, several sites were involved for their second or third year and were becoming more confident in implementing the program. Teams began to forge new directions, abandoning efforts that had little success, modifying their practices, and incorporating different approaches. CEC trainers encouraged teams to adapt the model and workshops to the needs of the school and the population. Flexibility and adaptation are significant aspects of the *Families and Schools* model and are crucial in the process of strengthening parent support practices. The almost exclusive format of "workshops" gave way to a much greater variety of activities, many of them primarily social, that established informal contact and trust between families and the schools. Child care, initially provided as a service so that parents could attend workshops, became more of a focus in itself and sites tried more activities in which parents and children were involved together. Some all-school events were added that focused on cultural diversity and programs were created for groups that were perceived to have special needs. Much wider staff involvement was evident and teams expanded.

In an evaluation of the programs operating in a variety of school sites, CEC gathered information on *what works* by asking schools to respond to a series of questions describing *what they did* and *the results they obtained*. The topics included recruitment, child care, content and conduct (organization), maintenance (funding/support), and staff participation. From this information (often augmented by samples of publicity, handouts, newspaper articles), the evaluator identified the variety of approaches that had been used. School sites also recorded basic statistics such as number of parents and children attending and frequency, race, primary language, economic status, and gender. It was useful for schools to conduct self-evaluation, to examine their practices in reaching all parents, especially groups that had not been active in school affairs. This information led to new strategies for reaching parents who had not participated. CEC used the evaluations to refine the training program and materials, incorporating successful strategies that could be implemented at replication sites. The project continued to grow serving 2300 parents in 1992-93 and over 5000 in 1993-94. Most of the programs are in elementary schools and are being piloted in middle schools.

Families and Schools: Powerful Partners, as implemented in Washington State, grew to be a dynamic network of participating schools. School teams attended trainings three times each year sharing successes, information, insights, and resources. Building on the tested methods of other teams and "borrowing" good ideas enabled all teams to maximize their learning and to improve their planning and implementation at a rapid rate. This cross-team training and exchange is viewed as one of the significant factors in the program's success and a goal for schools replicating the model. Beginning with one or two schools from the same district at pilot sites, teams can mentor new teams in the second and third years.

In Washington State, district-level sponsorship occurred as more schools in the same district became involved. Sponsorship resulted in district-level training in parent involvement, more diversity of membership, release time for teachers, and substantial business support. Within three years, one participating school served as a catalyst to engage another 17 schools, gained broad district and community support, and enlisted a business partner for each school. In this case, a long-term vision, strong leadership, and a successful program model resulted in a true demonstration of school-home-community partnership.

Program Outcomes

In the first seven years of participation in *Families and Schools: Powerful Partners*, children and families, educators, citizens, and the community have experienced positive results.

In 1988

- Tape series introduces native Spanish parents to Special Education and Individual Education Plans.
- Program expands from three communities in eastern Washington to urban and rural districts throughout the state.

In 1989

- Many bilingual and "newly arrived" families participate in school programs for the first time.
- Immigrant participants advocate for the continuation of parent outreach and education programs in a letter-writing campaign.
- Teachers encourage parent participation at home by restructuring their school's math curriculum to include *Home-Learning Activities*.

In 1990

- School sites report a 50% increase in numbers of parent and community volunteers.

- The number of parent requests for special programs and services for their children increases by 30%.
- "Kidhood" photoactivity cards are produced in English and Spanish for parents of infants, toddlers, and school-age children.

In 1991

- Schools begin to produce newsletters, handouts, and invitations in the home languages of the families they serve.
- By providing simultaneous workshops in English and Spanish, one school is able to increase Native American and Hispanic parent participation by 60% within one year.
- A participating school with strong district support receives a donated bus which is remodeled to provide structured parent-child activity sessions on the local military base. Donated equipment and materials are received from many sources to complete this project.

In 1992

- From one urban school, 20% of the teachers voluntarily do home visits prior to the start of the school year.

- After encouraging teachers to communicate regularly with families, schools show a 40% increase in positive communications from school to home.

- Over 2300 parents participate in school-sponsored evening workshops and family nights.

- A school with 97% student turnover per year notes a distinct shift in community support for the school following their outreach efforts. After two years, voters consistently approve school levies by a margin of 60%. School levies had previously been rejected 80% against to 20% in favor.

In 1993

- One full day of cultural diversity training is added to the training each school receives through *Families and Schools: Powerful Partners*.

- District level replication increases participation from 40% to 80% of all elementary schools in the district.

- *Families and Schools: Powerful Partners* is piloted at the middle school and junior high levels.

- Local business sponsors provide support of $500 for each of 18 schools.

- Partnerships are formed between schools and community organizations including grocery stores, restaurants, discount stores, senior centers, civic clubs, banks, and a shelter for homeless women and children.

- Diversity of school teams increases in race and ethnic membership from 8% to 29%.

In 1994

- Schools increase outreach to families whose children are bussed to a neighborhood 5 to 10 miles from their home.

- Quarterly newsletter and state-wide network are added to training component of *Families and Schools: Powerful Partners*.

- One urban, first year *Families and Schools* team produces a video about their school including narrative in English, Cambodian, and Vietnamese.

- Washington state legislature includes language and incentives to encourage parent involvement in its education reform package.

- District requests for information on the *Families and Schools* model increased by 70%.

Though the structure, materials, and emphasis of *Families and Schools: Powerful Partners* have evolved and changed since its inception in 1986, the program philosophy is the same—to increase student success by involving and empowering families. Empowerment is a crucial concept in the long-term process of strengthening the school-home relationship. To *empower*, according to the *American Heritage Dictionary* is "to authorize, enable, or permit." Schools have traditionally held the "power" and authority in education with parents and children doing what teachers and principals thought best.

Until recently, teachers had sole responsibility for educating children and schools functioned with little or no specific support or involvement from home. Communication with parents occurred infrequently, usually when the teacher had a child with a behavior problem or when parents were invited to school to attend an open house or school performance. Parents who were involved more directly did so through the PTA activities. In order to create a balance of authority and power between parents and educators, schools must be willing to share with parents the role of educating their children. And although we are realizing the value of collaboration, the partnership between home and school will not change simply because we know it's a good idea. Parent involvement policies at the school and district levels are becoming more common, but policies do not necessarily result in changes in behavior or attitudes. Parents' and teachers' perceptions of their roles are still based in the historical context.

Making the shift toward parent empowerment is not always easy, but it is fairly simple. Teachers and administrators can actively begin the process of empowering parents by affirming the strengths of each family, by respecting and trusting parents' insights into their child's needs and behavior, and by listening to and acting on the suggestions of parents and guardians. The concept of empowerment underlies the *Families and Schools: Powerful Partners* four core beliefs.

▷   **Every child needs and can benefit from supportive adults at home and at school working together on the child's behalf.**

▷   **When families and community are involved in the educational process, children do better in school and the quality of schools improves.**

▷   **All families have strengths to share and can support the school and their children's learning when offered opportunities to get involved in meaningful ways.**

▷   **Strong leadership skills and cooperative working relationships are necessary to implement and maintain an effective program that involves parents/guardians as full partners in education.**

The philosophy or core beliefs are the foundation for the *Families and Schools* program goals. The program provides the structure, format, strategies, and materials that enable a school/community to empower parents and families and to engage them as active educational partners.

The *Families and Schools: Powerful Partners* Goals

To improve communication and strengthen relationships between school and home, especially with those families who face multiple barriers to participation.

To increase the ability of parents and guardians to assist their children's learning at home and at school by expanding their knowledge and skills and improving access to school and community resources.

To engage businesses, social and health service agencies, and concerned citizens in actively supporting school efforts to involve all families in their children's education.

By communicating the importance of parent involvement and by providing options for parent participation, educators can create and enhance family-school partnerships. School leaders can demonstrate that parent involvement is not limited to attending an event, or volunteering for the bake sale or field trips, or joining the PTA, or serving on the site council. Parent involvement is all these things and much more.

A principal recently gave the best description of the Families and Schools philosophy when he said, What we're talking about is expanding the school's boundaries to create community. This is an ongoing process of building trust and relationship.

The *Families and Schools: Powerful Partners* model builds on the cumulative experiences of school teams over a period of seven years and reflects the best of what we know about how to create and maintain an effective school-home partnership. Based on these experiences, Citizens Education Center has concluded that three key actions are required for a successful school-wide parent involvement program.

▶ **Establish a team with the principal's leadership to gain support from the school and community.**

▶ **Make parent involvement an integral part of a school-wide process for improvement.**

▶ **Recognize the crucial role teachers play in establishing, building, and sustaining positive relationships with families.**

Establishing a School Team and Gaining Community Support

Research and validation of parent support efforts has confirmed that a team collaborative is needed to create, build, and sustain the important changes that strengthen family involvement in education. To implement change requires an enormous effort and is dependent on the "buy-in" of all stakeholders. In our experience, schools that attempt to streamline this process—to delegate the responsibilities of the team to a few teachers or to hire someone to serve as the sole "parent involvement coordinator"—report less success in achieving school-wide commitment, fail to achieve high percentages of diverse participation, and are less likely to sustain a family involvement effort for more than one year.

The team structure enables a school to implement effective parent involvement activities, but it is the support from school staff, district personnel, and local citizens that enables a successful parent program to maintain itself over time—to grow and to thrive. A diverse and representative school team supported by the school district and the community can guarantee all families greater access to the information and resources necessary to support school-home partnerships. Parents need support from teachers, teachers need support from the principal, and the principal needs support from the district supervisors. In Washington State, the most outstanding successes have occurred when visible support and tangible resources are consistently made available to parents, teachers, and team members from the school district and the local business community. The *Families and Schools* team approach and process recognizes and employs the unique skills and perspectives of *all* team members to coordinate, develop, and sustain resources for *all* children and their families.

Involving Parents and Creating Changes

Consistently affirmed in our experience is the fact that parents care about their children and want them to do well in school. They are eager to meet their children's teachers and to find out how they can be supportive at home. To do this, parents and guardians need information about the school's operating structure and classroom activities as well as specific ideas for participation.

Valuing and involving parents and guardians as educational partners is one aspect of improving schools and creating positive change. Making a commitment to involve parents more actively in the school requires consideration of the beliefs and attitudes about parent involvement held by teachers, parents, and students, and an answer to the question, Why and how should parents be involved in education? It requires examination of school facilities and policies and sensitivity to the message communicated regarding respect for parents and their presence in school.

Some of the assumptions and expectations surrounding parent participation are culturally determined. Awareness of the cultural beliefs and values related to education and school-home relationships is crucial to appropriate and effective communication with diverse families. Diversity includes socio-economic level, education, age, religion, race, and lifestyle. Acknowledging the need to include diverse perspectives brings both opportunity and challenge.

To maximize the opportunity to create positive school change, school administrators, teachers, parents, and concerned citizens must identify the changes that are necessary, take ownership of the changes that are planned, and participate actively in the change process. Change will affect everyone in the school and everyone will not accept change in the same way. Through its evaluation process, *Families and Schools* assists the team in understanding and implementing school change and growing in the process. The team's ability to sustain itself will depend on members' ability and willingness to learn from successes and disappointments and to realize satisfaction in their efforts.

Recognizing Teachers and Supporting Relationships

Teachers have a powerful influence on parent participation at school. When a teacher personally reaches out to a parent or guardian, that person is much more likely to come to the school. When parents and teachers can achieve mutually informative, trusting, and respectful partnerships, their combined ability to encourage positive growth and development in children is greatly enhanced.

Teachers want and need the support of parents. In order to work as partners with parents, they need information about the benefits of parent involvement, adequate time to develop relationships, and ideas to engage parents in meaningful ways. In the *Families and Schools* model, all team members focus their efforts to support, encourage, and strengthen the relationships between teachers, parents/guardians, and children.

I thought parents didn't have time to be involved. It turns out we didn't know what to expect from each other.

A Teacher

FAMILIES AND SCHOOLS *POWERFUL PARTNERS*

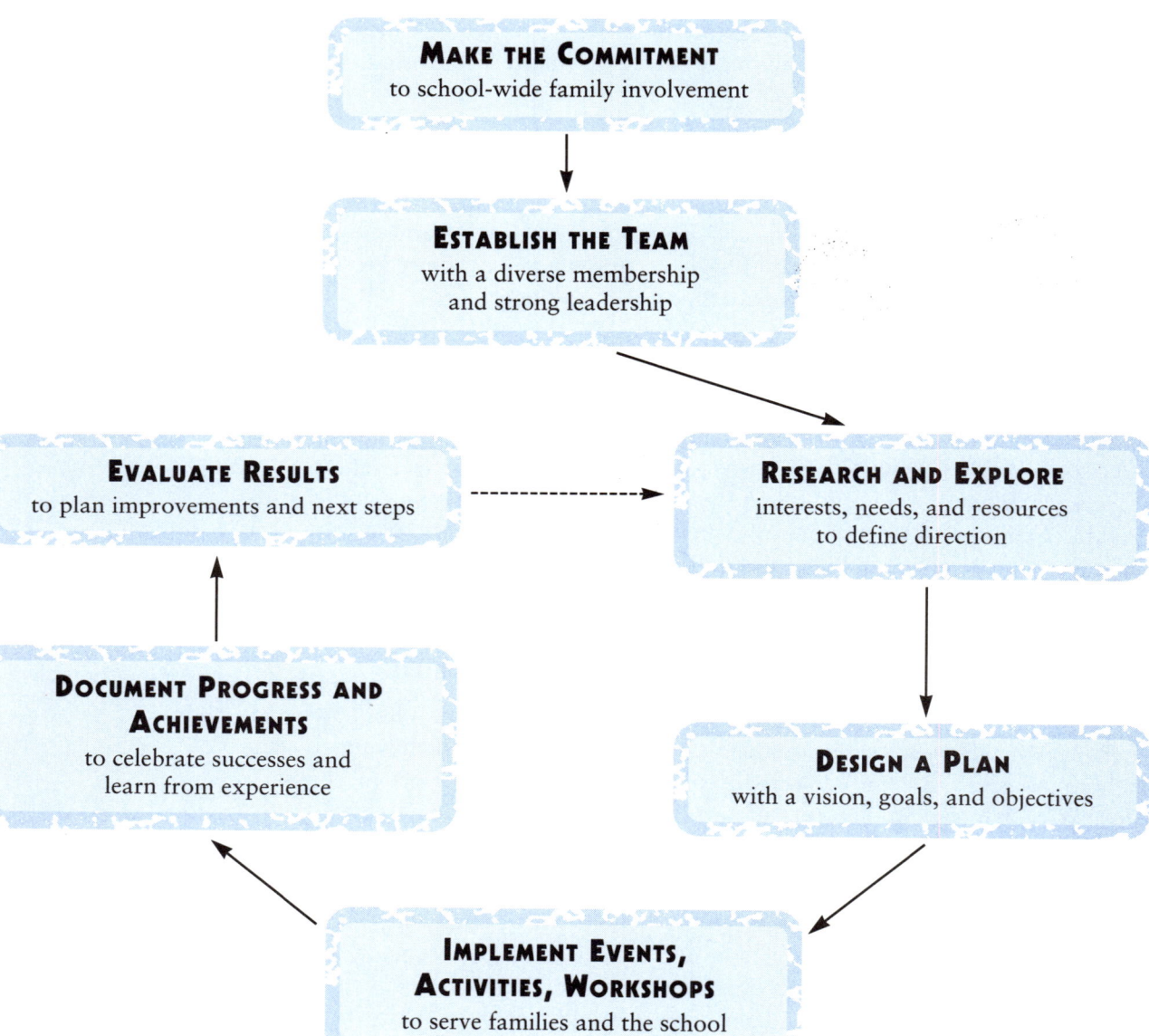

MAKE THE COMMITMENT
to school-wide family involvement

ESTABLISH THE TEAM
with a diverse membership
and strong leadership

EVALUATE RESULTS
to plan improvements and next steps

RESEARCH AND EXPLORE
interests, needs, and resources
to define direction

DOCUMENT PROGRESS AND ACHIEVEMENTS
to celebrate successes and
learn from experience

DESIGN A PLAN
with a vision, goals, and objectives

IMPLEMENT EVENTS, ACTIVITIES, WORKSHOPS
to serve families and the school

DEVELOPING THE TEAM

- ▷ **LEADERSHIP AND DIVERSITY**

- ▷ **ROLES AND RESPONSIBILITIES**

- ▷ **IDENTITY AND VISIBILITY**

The team's primary purpose is to provide leadership to the school—to bring families in as partners in education. The team functions as a steering committee to plan and coordinate family involvement activities. The team's efforts are developed around five major goals.

The Team's Goals

Assess the school's current outreach efforts to families.

Determine the needs and interests of parents/guardians.

Identify school, district, and community resources.

Coordinate school-wide plans.

Evaluate the outcomes of events and activities.

The team should represent all stakeholders, including parents, teachers, a principal or administrator, a business representative, a social or health service representative, and a cultural or language specialist. In order to achieve success in reaching all segments of the population, the team composition must reflect the racial, ethnic, and economic diversity represented in the student population and their families. *Diversity* in this chapter means inclusion of all stakeholders—individuals with different roles related to children and with different backgrounds and/or perspectives. Each team member brings an important and unique perspective that contributes to the program's success.

Each team needs a leader—someone who initiates, oversees, and develops the team; who makes sure that the planning process happens and that plans get implemented. The team leader is usually the principal, but may be a teacher, a counselor, or a parent who works closely with the principal. As initiator of the *Families and Schools* team, the leader identifies potential team members and begins the recruitment process. As overseer of the planning process, the leader schedules planning sessions, creates the agenda, and facilitates the meetings. S/he ensures that the team is well organized and collaborates with teachers and parents, school and community groups in planning program activities. The leader ensures that all team members have the information, skills, and time necessary to fulfill their responsibilities and to participate actively in order to sustain the program over time.

Identifying Team Members

Excellent team candidates are action-oriented individuals willing to "do what it takes" to accomplish a goal. They understand the significance of parent involvement in student success and are committed to increasing that involvement. They appreciate and reflect the diversity of the school community and see differences as opportunities for learning. Team members should be capable of clear communication between the team and its various constituencies.

The ideal first-year team is eight to ten individuals who are currently involved in outreach or advocacy efforts with families. Teachers participating in outreach efforts are strong candidates because they contribute experience and ideas to the team. Bilingual faculty, school staff, and teaching assistants should also be considered for the team. Parent team members should include at least one person who is already active in the PTA/PTO, on the site-based management team, or who is a classroom volunteer. The team should include at least two parent/guardians representative of the school population, for example, bilingual parents, parents from various ethnic groups, those whose children live outside the school/neighborhood, or parents with children who are physically and intellectually challenged.

The recruitment process can begin at meetings of the faculty and staff, PTA/ PTO, school committee, and community groups. The principal or team leader explains the importance of building school-home-community partnerships and introduces the *Families and Schools* program to create interest in the program and to motivate people to get involved. A personal invitation from the principal to join the school's commitment to parent involvement helps to solidify commitments to the team.

The Principal

As the educational leader, the principal creates a base of support for the team and articulates school-home partnership as a top priority.

Without a supportive and committed principal, a school atmosphere that welcomes parents and citizens is not likely to happen. The principal must have a strong personal belief that parents and community members can help the school achieve a positive learning environment for *all* children. S/he must regard family involvement as an integral part of the school's services. After providing support and articulating the vision, the most significant action the principal can take is to become an active member of the team, assuming an equal share of the team's responsibilities. Working alongside teachers, parents, and community members, the principal can send a strong and visible message regarding his/her belief in the importance of school, family, and community collaboration for student success.

Teachers

Through their interaction with families, teachers are acutely aware of the importance of family support in assuring a child's school success.

Teachers should be invited to assist as Workshop presenters, to provide the primary communication between school and home, and to invite parents to

Workshops and events. Teachers and special needs staff may also take leadership roles in developing *Home-Learning Activities* that relate to the school curriculum and integrating those activities into the school-wide family involvement plan. (For additional information, see Chapter Four, *Planning for Success* and *Workshops for Families and Educators*.)

Parents/Guardians

Parents help to identify and communicate family needs and offer practical suggestions so that team plans relate to the needs and interests of all families.

Parents function as equal participants in the planning, implementation, and evaluation of team efforts. Parent members of the team may serve as role models for other less involved parents/guardians. One successful outcome of the *Families and Schools* team model is the opportunity for parents to grow into leadership roles in the school. Many previously uninvolved parents have attended team-sponsored events, then gradually moved into more active roles such as joining the team, assisting teachers in classrooms, working with the PTA/PTO, becoming paid parent coordinators, or joining the site council.

Cultural Specialists and Interpreters

Cultural specialists contribute an awareness and sensitivity that enhances team efforts.

Their understanding of different cultural assumptions and expectations helps the team create an environment where *all* families feel comfortable and welcome. Interpreters are important team members because they can provide essential information to non-English-speaking families. Their participation also encourages others to recognize the diversity and richness that various racial and ethnic groups contribute to the school.

Community or Business Representative

When citizens and business owners see a correlation between school success and business/community growth, they welcome opportunities to collaborate with the school.

As part of the team, the community representative provides a unique perspective on how to enlist the support and help of the larger community to strengthen school-home relationships. His/her organization can assist in obtaining funds, help businesses encourage employees to volunteer for mentoring and tutoring, and help parents get release time to volunteer and participate in school events. Community representatives can also be invited to participate as facilitators, presenters, and financial contributors. Businesses that have participated in Washington State include major banks, supermarkets, and department stores. Organizations include ministerial associations, the Rotary Club, the Kiwanis Club, a shelter for homeless women and children, senior citizen groups, and local churches.

Social or Health Service Representative

Social and health service representatives are effective presenters at workshops as well as strong community advocates for the school's family involvement program.

These representatives may include school district staff, family support workers, counselors, school psychologists, public health or nursing professionals, doctors, and family therapists. Because of their direct contact with families, they have established a level of trust that enables them to reach out to alienated or disenfranchised families and provide insights for involving families who face multiple barriers to participation.

 ## ROLES AND RESPONSIBILITIES

Team functions and members' responsibilities vary in each school depending upon the specific goals and objectives set. Shared responsibility is necessary because tremendous energy is required to initiate and sustain the school-home partnership effort. The team will be most effective if all members guard against burnout, which can occur if one person or a few assume all the responsibility. Each team member should become familiar with the information in this *Guide*. (Chapters Three, Four, and Five and *Resources* contain information necessary to define the scope of potential accomplishments.)

Team members choose their responsibilities within the context of the team's goals and objectives. Team members have found a variety of ways to share these responsibilities by assuming one or two roles for the school year, by sharing a task with another member, or by rotating roles for each event. Some teams find it helpful to delegate specific responsibilities using a task description format. Experience indicates that roles are easier as members become familiar with the skills required for the tasks. It is suggested that the team coordinate the main tasks for each member's role using an outline such as the following. (See *Team Members' Roles and Responsibilities* and *Team Member List* in *Resources*.)

Communications Coordinator

- Notifies appropriate media about family involvement activities.
- Provides information to the faculty and staff about program goals, events and Workshops including agenda, location, date, and time.
- Makes informative presentations at staff meetings, community meetings, open house, PTA/PTO meetings.

Invitation Coordinator

- Coordinates personal phone calls to targeted families.
- Finds translators to communicate with families in their home languages.
- Creates and displays posters announcing events for the school and community.
- Writes and makes copies of invitations to distribute in classrooms.

Child Care Coordinator

- Coordinates developmentally appropriate child care for family nights.
- Arranges logistics and registration for child care.
- Finds adequate numbers of qualified adults to provide child care.

Workshop Facilitator

- Welcomes, affirms, rewards, and recognizes all families.
- Conducts the Workshops through the scheduled agenda and provides guidance for small group work.
- Takes appropriate action to address the concerns, questions, and suggestions that arise at the Workshops.

Logistics Coordinator

- Makes building and room arrangements for Family Night events.
- Prepares and displays locator signs inside and outside the building.
- Responds to transportation needs of families.
- Coordinates preparation of meals and/or snacks.

Finance and Budgeting Coordinator

- Assists the team in raising money to cover Workshop expenses.
- Monitors income and expenses; informs team regarding finances.

Materials Coordinator

- Buys or solicits donations, supplies, and materials for team events.
- Prepares any written flyers or handouts for workshops.
- Assists data collector with sign-in and registration forms.

Historian

- Assists with planning, narrating, and taping videos of the school setting for parent audiences.
- Arranges for photographs or videos to be taken of Family Night activities.
- Sets up visual wall displays in the school following each event.
- Provides and posts a list of the families and staff who attended each event.

Data Collector 1*

- Determines data collection methods to be used.
- Collects sign-in sheets from registration.
- Designs a plan for assigning and tracking return of *Home-Learning Activities*.
- Writes up notes on the session.

*For data collection, it is recommended that the same one or two team members be responsible for the full school year. The task requires time to become familiar with the various data collection instruments and to be consistent when gathering and collating this information.

Data Collector 2

- Works with Data Collector 1 to gather appropriate information.
- Completes *Attendance Worksheet* using sign-in sheets and *Annual School Profile*.
- Reports findings to the team during the next planning session.

Setting Goals and Organizing for Teamwork

The team leader facilitates the process to set goals and organize the team to work together effectively and efficiently. The following topics and questions may be used to guide the planning. (See also *Resources*.)

Goal-Setting

- How will the team address the major goals of the program?
- What does the team plan to accomplish this year? next year? in three years?
- How will team members use their roles to accomplish these goals?

Implementation

- Where, when, and how often will the team meet?
- Who will facilitate the team meetings? If there are co-chairs, what are their functions? Will the facilitation responsibilities be rotated?
- How and when will meeting agendas be set?

Communication

- How will team members gather responses from their constituents?
- How will team members report back to their constituents?
- How will team members communicate with each other between meetings?

Documentation

- What is the procedure for recording and summarizing meeting minutes?
- Who will be responsible for gathering and disseminating information?
- What other record-keeping is needed and how will it be maintained?

Assessment

- What measures will team member use to assess their progress?
- How will the team incorporate results and feedback into future planning?

IDENTITY AND VISIBILITY

If a school's parent involvement effort is to grow and sustain itself, the team must create a unique identity to distinguish itself from other school groups or teams. In order to achieve visibility within the school and in the surrounding community, the team needs a name. Names chosen by teams in Washington State include F.A.S.T. (Families and Schools Together), S.H.I.P. (Schools and Homes in Partnership), T.I.E. (Together in Education), Family Connections, and Partners for Success. Some teams have chosen the name *Families and Schools: Powerful Partners* or simply *Powerful Partners*.

To reinforce identity and visibility, use ideas that develop consistency.

- Use the team name in all communications.
- Design a logo and use it on all correspondence.
- Display signs that introduce the team in highly visible locations at school.
- Create T-Shirts for the team to wear at events.
- Use the same color paper for all printed information.
- Plan activities on a regular schedule of day and time.

Once the team is assembled and has established guidelines for organizing and working together, members are ready to begin the actions that bring this program to life. Chapters Three, Four, and Five describe the process that is summarized in **L.E.A.D.E.R.S.H.I.P.**

The program's long-term success in any school or district depends upon the team's ability to individualize—to take ownership of the program. It is important for each team to build on the enthusiasm and ideas of individual members. All members and participants should be encouraged to contribute new ideas and to suggest ways to adapt those presented. Teams should be realistic in their expectations and aware that establishing strong school-home partnerships and an environment that is comfortable for families is a one-to three-year process. (See *One Year Calendar of Team Activities* in *Resources*.)

SUMMARY

Leadership from the principal and a diverse team of teachers, parents, and citizens are necessary to create, build, and sustain a school-home partnership.

Shared responsibility, well-defined roles, clear expectations, and flexibility contribute to an organized, productive team.

Team visibility and a unique identity will help to generate interest and gather support for the team's efforts, thus increasing the potential for long-term success.

It has been fun—so much fun to work on a team!

Community Representative

Learn about your family population and their needs. Learn together how to build relationships with all families.

Explain to all staff and faculty what the team is doing and why. Let them know specifically how they can participate.

Advocate for parent and community involvement within your school and at the district level. Ask about funding available for parent involvement.

Develop plans and schedule activities to involve families in a variety of interesting and significant ways.

Express to all families your desire to work with them as equal partners in the education of their child/ren.

Reflect on what you have accomplished. Record what worked and what didn't. Remember to celebrate!

Seek input from parents at events regarding topics of interest. Respond to those suggestions in a visible and timely manner.

Help kids get excited about events at school and they will motivate their parents to attend. Helpful Hints: FOCUS, FOOD, FUN!

Integrate *FSPP* activities with Chapter 1, PTA/PTO, Head Start and ESL. Institutionalize your team's efforts through visibility and consistency.

Present your team's objectives and successes at meetings of the staff, site council, PTA, and local citizen groups and organizations.

L.E.A.D.E.R.S.H.I.P.

BUILDING A STRONG FOUNDATION

> ⌵ **RELATIONSHIPS AND COMMUNICATION**
>
> ⌵ **BARRIERS AND BRIDGES**
>
> ⌵ **COORDINATION AND SUPPORT**

The *Families and Schools: Powerful Partners* model recognizes that the most effective way to increase support for school children is to improve and strengthen the interrelationships of those who have the greatest impact on children and their learning. The team's activities bring opportunities to increase trust and respect and to open new channels of communication between teachers, parents/guardians, and children. Building a strong foundation is a long-term process that begins by recognizing and valuing parents and their role as equal participants in their children's education.

To build and strengthen partnerships between school and home requires that the team focus on specific strategies.

Strategies

- Use adequate and effective methods and practices of communication.

- Identify barriers to participation and ways to overcome them.

- Coordinate efforts within the school to involve parents.

- Secure support for the team from the district and the community.

Positive communication is the *key* to developing strong partnerships. For example, informal conversations between teachers and parents/guardians that focus on the child's strengths, talents, and special qualities rather than on concerns and problems convey the teacher's respect for the parent, care for the child, and interest in a reciprocal relationship. Communication between school and home must be two-way. *Effective* communication involves *listening* as well as telling. Staff members need to demonstrate that they are listening and that parent input affects their actions. The most effective communication is face to face; the second most effective is the telephone. It has been proven that written communication is not an effective substitute for personal contact and therefore should be used to supplement personal contact when requesting parent participation at school events.

In order to participate effectively in their children's education, parents say they want and need **information, relationships,** and **ideas.**

> Parents want *information* about how the school operates and conducts activities; they want information about the curriculum and the learning environment; they want to know how children are evaluated, the standards for achievement, about daily routines, and the expectations for behavior. They want to know about school programs and opportunities for their children's participation. They want information about school personnel and their responsibilities.

▶ Parents want one-to-one *relationships* with teachers, support staff, and the principal. They want opportunities to meet and talk with teachers, to work with the school to enhance their children's achievements, and to discuss concerns before they become problems. Frequent communications between school and home establish a basis for mutual respect that allows parents to ask questions, to provide insight into their child's unique needs and challenges, and to become partners with the school in problem-solving.

▶ Parents want specific *ideas* about what they can do at home to support classroom learning, how to be proactive in preventing learning problems, and how to support the teacher's direction and guidance. Parents are eager to learn techniques and strategies that encourage children's motivation to learn and succeed.

The *Families and Schools* team empowers parents through Workshops and other events and in interviews and surveys by providing opportunities for parents to ask questions, raise issues, and make suggestions. These methods are discussed in detail in Chapter Four, *Planning for Success*.

Responding to parents' questions and suggestions builds trust, establishes a system for dialogue between school and home, and demonstrates the school's willingness to listen and value parents' ideas. Effective responses include posting parent concerns and the school's responses on a bulletin board or in the school newsletter or in a follow-up telephone call to the parent/guardian who raised the concern or made the suggestion. A timely response from a teacher, the principal, or another team member sends a message that parent/guardian input is welcome and given serious consideration.

In addition to its role in building relationships, communication is critical in overcoming barriers that prevent family participation in schools. *(See next section)*.

I learned how to ask questions...I got answers.

A Parent

To increase the potential for a strong family involvement program, teams must identify and overcome barriers to participation and establish structures and routines that prevent further barriers from developing.

The team's challenge is to address, reduce, or eliminate any obstacles it can in order to achieve maximum participation. These challenges can be met with a variety of strategies.

Strategies

- Personally invite parents to participate.

- Offer options and opportunities for participation.

- Make special arrangements that enable parents/guardians and teachers to attend events and activities, for example, offer meals, child care, transportation, and language interpretation.

- Set a goal to get all families to participate in some way.

- Redefine a "good parent turnout" to mean success in reaching diverse populations and families of developmentally challenged children.

- Overcome prior negative experiences by making everyone feel welcome and comfortable.

- Identify and use behaviors that increase parents' trust and confidence in the school.

There are many reasons why parents are reluctant to come to school and there are also factors that prevent teachers from seeking parents as educational partners. By acknowledging the common barriers to participation such as time pressures, lack of child care, and conflicting priorities, the team can create a structure that appeals to even the busiest families. Some of the obstacles that prevent attendance or participation are reflected in statements from parents/guardians and school staff. This section examines these obstacles and makes recommendations to avoid or overcome them.

Barriers

Parent

I know this meeting at school is important, but I can't afford to hire a sitter again and I feel bad about not spending time with my kids in the evening.

Teacher

This is the third evening meeting this week. I'm here all day with other people's children, and I never have time to spend with my own family.

Bridges

Offer free or inexpensive child care during workshops. Schedule time during the evening for families to be together in addition to separate planned time for children and adults. Encourage teachers to bring their families to family-night activities.

Barriers

Parent

Joey's mom just told me there's a meeting at school tonight. Were you supposed to bring me some information about it?

Oh, sorry, Dad—I forgot. Here it is. (A wrinkled piece of paper from the bottom of the backpack.)

Well, it starts in twenty minutes and we haven't had dinner yet, so I guess I'll have to skip this one.

Principal

We put a notice in the school bulletin last week and sent out a flyer on Thursday. I can't understand why so few people came to a meeting this important.

Bridges

Do not assume that written information will be received or read. Make personal contacts or follow written information with a phone call. Describe in detail the purpose, activities, and schedule for the meeting or event and why it is important. Communicate in advance to allow ample time for families to plan attendance.

Barriers

Parent

I wouldn't mind helping out, but there seems to be an expectation that I volunteer in the classroom or serve on the school improvement committee. I work during the day and I feel out of place in those school meetings. They talk about all kinds of things I don't understand. Sometimes all the letters and acronyms sound like another language.

Teacher

There is so much to do every day with 32 children in my class that I end up taking a lot of work home at night. I could ask a parent to volunteer in the classroom, but it seems to make my job harder because then I have to find something for the parent to do on top of everything else. Besides, it makes me nervous to know they are watching and judging me.

Bridges

Students and teachers can benefit from additional help and many parents want to help. Volunteering in the classroom or serving on committees are not the only ways to make a difference. Offer a variety of options including activities parents/guardians can do at home to help their children and the teachers.

Researchers have determined that the type of parent involvement activity having the most significant effect on students' learning is doing activities at home that correspond to the school curriculum. Emphasize fun activities that can be done in 15-20 minutes.

Barriers

Co-parent

I feel uncomfortable going to meetings at the school, even though I'm very interested in what goes on there. Sometimes I'm the only man in the room, and I also get the feeling that people are judging me because I'm not Lakisha's real father and Sonia and I aren't married.

School Counselor

Based on our meeting attendance, it's clear that fathers are just not interested in what goes on at school. That one man has come a couple of times, but I'm not even sure who he is.

Bridges

Get to know who the significant adults are in each student's life. Help them get to know and feel comfortable with you (teacher, team member). Sponsor activities that appeal to men and fathers. Encourage the attendance of co-parents, guardians, and other members of the child's family with personal invitations.

Barriers

Parent

I'm overwhelmed enough by having to get Lenora from day care, make the kids something for dinner, deal with their homework, and try to get everyone in bed at a decent hour. Staying out late on a school night is out of the question.

Teacher

I'm exhausted from the day, need to pick up Shawn from child care, grab another fast food meal, and make it back here for the meeting. I guess I'll work on my lesson plans after the kids go to sleep.

Bridges

Offer a simple, nutritious meal for parents, children, and school staff prior to family night workshop activities and other events. Conclude evening activities by 8:00 or 8:30 P.M. Open the school at 5 P.M. with options for homework help and use of the library prior to 6 P.M. dinner and workshop.

Barriers

Foster Parent

The last thing I need is to go to a meeting tonight. I sit in meetings all day at work. I just want to go home and relax. Anyway, I'm sure no one will miss me if I'm not there.

Teacher

I was planning to come back for the meeting, but my kids want to stay home. Their favorite show is on TV tonight. I just don't have the energy to argue with them about it.

Bridges

Plan events that are relaxing and fun. Get children involved as presenters or performers. Make specific requests of individual parents and teachers so that everyone has a role to play and knows others are depending on him/her.

Barriers

Parent

I work hard at being a good parent and I resent the attitude of some of those teachers that I'm doing everything wrong. I never did like school, and I'm sure not going to go there just to have them preach at me about how to raise my kids.

Teacher

I work hard at being a good teacher of children and I don't want to have to teach their parents, too. I resent being made to feel guilty if I don't choose to come back to school for meetings several nights a week.

Bridges

Organize unstructured opportunities for parents and teachers to be together informally and have fun. Make attendance voluntary, but provide incentives that make participation very attractive. Eliminate the pressure to be the perfect parent or the perfect teacher and many negative feelings will be overcome.

Barriers

Grandparent

My English is not so good. I get shy talking in a group and feel atontado *(embarrassed or foolish) so I don't go to the school meetings.*

Principal

We never see Paulo's grandparents at school events. I guess they're just not interested in what goes on at this school.

Bridges

Extend personal invitations to school events in the family's home language. Enlist bilingual staff or community members to interpret during a meeting or hold a separate session for families who are non-English speaking. Allow older children to stay with their parents and interpret for them until parents feel comfortable.

Barriers

Parent

I can't wait until I have a decent car that isn't always breaking down. I've missed three meetings at school because I don't like taking the bus at night, and I really can't afford a taxi plus child care.

Principal

It's unfortunate that so many of the parents whose children arrive by school bus don't come to our evening events. Some of them have never even seen the school their children attend.

Bridges

Arrange transportation for parents who live in distant areas or who don't have transportation. Solicit funding from the PTA or community groups for transportation or ask a taxi company to donate services so that all parents can attend school events. Introduce parents to teachers or families who live in the area and encourage car pooling.

The Families and Schools experience has revealed many problems that impede the progress of a strong school-home partnership. Chapter Four, *Planning for Success,* outlines a process for identifying additional issues or barriers that impede school-home partnerships. Individual team assessment of the school population will reveal the more specific, personal barriers that need to be addressed. Once these barriers are identified, the team can take measures to overcome them and ensure that everyone who wants to participate can do so.

I've never met a parent who didn't care...I have met parents who didn't know how to help their children, but they all cared.

A Principal

To increase the potential for strong school-home partnerships, the team must seek and get broad support within the school and the community. The primary factors in achieving long-term support are communication and coordination.

In the planning stages, the team should identify the individuals and groups with whom the team will communicate and the team members responsible for communicating with constituents on a regular basis. Though the individuals and groups will vary from school to school, communication needs to occur within the school itself, at the district administration office, and in the surrounding community.

Within the school, team members should communicate with students, the counselor, classroom teacher, special needs and bilingual teachers, staff members including secretaries, the librarian, custodians, and other groups such as child care providers, Head Start teachers, the PTA, site council, or learning-improvement committee. At the district office, the team will meet with volunteer coordinators, public relations officers, Executive Directors, the Superintendent, and other central office staff who should be informed of and invited to the school's family involvement activities. School board members and staff from neighboring schools can be invited to attend or participate in some events.

Outreach to the community can include local business owners, civic organizations, news reporters and other local media personnel, churches, social clubs, senior citizen groups, immediate neighbors, community recreation centers, and social and health service agencies.

Coordinating Within the School

To prevent fragmentation of program offerings and to avoid duplication of services and competition for time from parents, teachers, and community members, it is helpful to coordinate all the parent involvement efforts at a school site under one "umbrella." The *Families and Schools* team may function in this capacity, accepting responsibility for overseeing and coordinating school-wide efforts to reach out to families. The parent involvement "umbrella" should facilitate connection between teachers and parents in all school programs, including Head Start, Special Education, Chapter 1, and Bilingual Education.

Incorporate into the school-wide plan the school's existing parent involvement activities such as Open House, parent-teacher conferences, PTA meetings, and classroom volunteer opportunities. Staff members who have regular contact with parents and families must be informed of and/or involved in activities sponsored by the *Families and Schools* team. Family support workers, child care providers, school secretaries, and bus drivers all have a unique perspective and a role to play in the family outreach effort. Chapter Four, *Planning for Success*, includes a process for identifying and coordinating school-wide resources.

To coordinate family involvement efforts effectively throughout the school, include a variety of strategies.

- Create a school-wide calendar of all events and activities to reach out to parents.

- Include representatives from various groups on the team.

- Publish a parent newsletter or install telephone recorded information for all the groups' activities.

- Encourage faculty, staff, and parents to share family involvement efforts at regular school meetings.

- Co-sponsor family involvement activities with PTA/PTO, Head Start, on-site or local child care programs, school improvement committees, and site council.

- Invite support staff to make presentations at workshops and provide input into the school-wide plan.

Involving the Faculty and School Staff

To generate interest and enthusiasm in the team's program, initiate professional awareness sessions that highlight the connection between parent involvement and children's academic success. Provide practical suggestions for classroom teachers to engage in family involvement practices. Identify teachers who have made a personal commitment to parent involvement and seek their leadership in broadening staff support. Involve teachers and staff in the early stages of program commitment and seek representatives from the entire school to be members of the team. Keep the teachers and staff informed about program goals and objectives, share documentation of program activities and outcomes, and encourage feedback from those who attend and participate in team-sponsored events. Ask people to fulfill specific, time-limited tasks rather than expressing a need for "any volunteers" or a general request that staff "get behind this effort." As stated earlier, teachers and other school staff are more likely to support the team and participate in parent involvement activities if the program has the visible support of the principal, if teachers are committed to involving parents, and if teacher participation is noticed and appreciated in some tangible way.

To encourage participation, plan to implement several strategies.

Strategies

- Offer a variety of specific roles for participation in family involvement events.

- Invite teachers to present and facilitate at events and workshops.

- Offer incentives such as compensation time or pay to participating staff members.

- Find creative, fun ways to acknowledge and show appreciation for staff involvement in the program.

Engaging the Community

To achieve outstanding results, schools need the support of local citizens and business owners.

When seeking community involvement, *partnership* is the key word.

▶ Local citizens need to understand why their involvement is important to the school's ability to meet the needs of children and families.

▶ Citizens need to be assured that the school staff values their input and wants them to participate.

▶ Citizens need specific options or opportunities for participation.

▶ Citizens need recognition and appreciation for their time and effort.

All levels of participation must be accepted with ongoing opportunities to contribute in large and small ways. Teams should include citizens representing the diversity of the community and work to establish long-term partnerships with local businesses and organizations for mutually beneficial results.

Community partnerships can be enhanced with specific strategies.

Strategies

- Establish connections by inviting community members to Workshops, events, and student performances.

- Ask businesses for their support. Remember that support takes many different forms. Be creative.

- Encourage community and business sponsorship of a specific event or program such as a multicultural fair or Workshop series or a certain aspect of the year's activities such as meals, transportation, or child care.

- Make requests that are consistent with the organization's purpose in the community. (For example, ask the local newspaper staff to provide free advertising space for the event or to publish an article featuring the school's family and community outreach efforts; ask the local bicycle shop to donate a bike or bike safety equipment as prizes for a raffle or drawing.)

- Provide documentation for businesses specifying the use of their financial contributions and explain how children and families benefited from their support.

- Introduce community supporters at events, acknowledge them in the school newsletter; ask students, families, and the staff to personally thank citizens for contributions.

The following is one school's story of progress in overcoming barriers and building a strong foundation for an ongoing family involvement effort.

Oakwood Elementary School serves more than 400 students in grades K–5. It is located in an unincorporated area outside a large city, an area that has traditionally had a high crime rate and very low socio-economic status. Many children who attend the school live in multi-unit housing that was built for the families of military personnel during World War II.

The school's population is 56% diversity: Asian 18%, African American 27%, Hispanic 7%, Native American 4%. Of the school population, 67% qualified for free or reduced lunch. The student turnover rate averages 75–90% each year. A large percentage of students live in single parent households. Parents tend to be transient, very isolated, and without reliable transportation.

Oakwood's family involvement program runs for eight weeks in the fall and eight weeks in the spring. Invitations are sent out in English, Korean, and Spanish. Each session begins with a meal in the cafeteria for all who attend joined by school staff. Tables are covered with butcher paper and supplied with crayons and markers. After dinner, parents and guardians go to an adult workshop and children go to child care. Workshops include a variety of topics chosen by parents and of interest to parents. The emphasis is on providing support and connection among families, thereby reducing isolation and stress.

In four years, Oakwood has changed from a school in which parents had little trust and sometimes open hostility towards school staff to one in which families say they feel welcome and their children are happy in an atmosphere that is warm and friendly. The school and community—suffering severe racial tensions—has changed to a school with an active program of acceptance and appreciation of cultural diversity. Each year, this school mobilizes thousands of hours of volunteer help from citizens and parents as well as thousands of dollars of direct financial contributions and donations.

The principal, faculty, and parents at Oakwood continue to deepen and expand their connections with all families and the community. Oakwood has proven that with the principal's leadership and a diverse team, with clear vision, a coordinated plan, and consistent effort over time, a school's culture can be powerfully transformed.

SUMMARY

Effective communication is necessary to establish trust and respect and to strengthen the relationships between teachers, parents/guardians, and children.

Meaningful interactions occur between families and schools when barriers to participation are identified and solutions are created to overcome the barriers.

Cooperation and support result when individuals and groups from the school, the district, and the community coordinate efforts to build a strong family involvement program.

In our transient population, it is especially important that parents have a place to connect with other parents, to share ideas and to realize common problems. They often gain solutions to problems from other parents or staff members, but sometimes it is enough to know they are not alone in their struggles with raising children.

School Counselor

PLANNING FOR SUCCESS

- ▹ **PROCESS AND VISION**

- ▹ **RESEARCH AND EXPLORATION**

- ▹ **DESIGN AND IMPLEMENTATION**

▷ PROCESS AND VISION

Families and Schools: Powerful Partners is structured for long-term commitment. Teams with a long-range perspective succeed because they clarify/modify goals as necessary in their progress and gain motivation and momentum by acknowledging and celebrating their accomplishments along the way. Because the process is long-term, it is crucial to set realistic goals. The *Three-Year Summary of a Team's Accomplishments* identifies the actual experiences of teams in Washington State and demonstrates the accomplishments possible using the *Families and Schools* model. (See *Guide Resources*.)

To create a plan that reaches for success, it is recommended that the *Families and Schools* team follow a *process*—a sequence of actions—that moves it closer to the chief goal of developing strong partnerships with families. In following this process, the team will focus on a central area of interest, will set and define goals and objectives, and will take actions to reach those goals and objectives.

Without a structured process and a clear focus, it is difficult to determine which of the many possible directions the team should take. A team might try a variety of ways and not realize if or how its initiatives made a difference or were worth the time and effort invested. By focusing on and taking a specific direction, the team will produce tangible results and feel satisfied and motivated to continue its efforts.

The *Families and Schools* Model

RESEARCH the needs and interests of the school and community.

▼

EXPLORE the resources and build on strengths and successes.

▼

DESIGN a plan to address the needs and interests of the school and community.

▼

IMPLEMENT the plan of workshops, activities, and events that strengthen relationships.

▼

DOCUMENT the progress and achievements.

▼

EVALUATE the results.

This chapter will describe the first four steps; Chapter Five, *Documenting Progress and Results*, is devoted to the last two steps of the process.

The team may begin by discussing what the members want to accomplish in a given period of time, for example, in three years.

- **How will the school be different?**

- **What will parents, teachers, and children see or hear as they enter the building that indicates strong school-home partnerships?**

- **How will it feel to be a part of the school?**

- **What kinds of communication will occur between parents/guardians and teachers?**

- **What kinds of support will be available to the school and families from citizens in the local community?**

This exchange of personal and team views, hopes, and aspirations can lead to a one-sentence statement that captures the essence of the team's vision. A vision energizes and inspires team members. Creating one is essential to developing a successful plan. Once the vision is articulated, the team will begin to focus on planned outcomes and to clarify goals and objectives.

These examples from *Families and Schools* teams may help to create team vision statements.

- The entire community believes, "This is *our* school!"

- This is a "belonging" kind of place, a "working it out" kind of place.

- Each child has several caring adults supporting his/her education.

- *All* families and *all* children have positive attitudes about this school, and feel comfortable and welcome here.

- The faculty of this school has cooperative, trusting relationships with parents and other members of the community.

- Parents and teachers respect and value each other as partners in children's education.

When the team has committed to following a structured process, created a vision, and gained understanding about what is reasonable to expect over a three-year period, it is ready to begin its family involvement action plan.

Now I understand that we have to determine what parent involvement means at our school and what we have to do to accomplish it.

A Team Member

The purpose of team research is to achieve awareness of the diverse makeup of the student body, school activities that currently involve parents and families, and current strengths and weaknesses in school-home communication. By investigating the current status of school-home relations and inquiring into existing resources, the team maximizes its capacity to create informed, appropriate, and realistic plans.

Initially, information will be gathered by the team, and recorded on several forms: *Annual School Profile, Qualities of Effective School-Home Partnerships,* and *Current Connections.* It is recommended that two or three members work together to complete the forms and then give a copy to each team member and discuss the responses at a planning session. The team may feel comfortable defining goals and objectives after reviewing these forms or may choose to gather additional data as described in the following sections of this chapter: *Expanding Data Collection* and *Exploring Strengths, Resources, and Opportunities for Improvement.*

Gathering Initial Information

Annual School Profile

Description A quantitative summary of information about the school—its size, organization and management, vision or mission, faculty and staff, students, and families

Function By exchanging this information during a team planning session, team members can begin the planning process with shared understanding and similar perspectives. This form should be completed early in the year and referred to as necessary. It is used to guide the team's planning and goal setting and as a basis for comparing family participation in workshops and events with the total school population.

Qualities of Effective School-Home Partnerships*

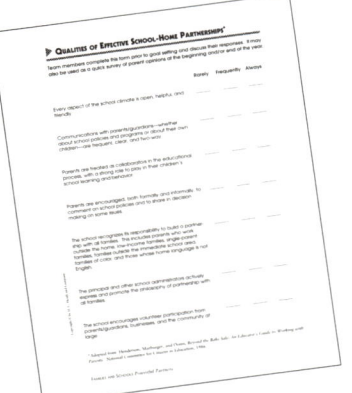

Description Insights into the components that comprise an effective school-home partnership effort and the school's current level of success in exhibiting these qualities

Function This form is used by the team primarily for discussion but can be used more broadly as a quick survey of staff members or parents. Teams have also found this form to be useful in gauging success of the parent involvement efforts over the course of the year by soliciting responses early in the year and comparing them to responses at the end of the school year.

*Adapted from Henderson, Marburger, and Ooms, *Beyond the Bake Sale: An Educator's Guide to Working with Parents.* National Committee for Citizens in Education, 1986.

Current Connections

Description Identifies current levels of parent/community/school involvement and support

Function Completed early in the school year, this form will provide baseline information on existing partnerships. When all team members share a common understanding about the current levels of partnership with families and the community, it is easier to focus on enhancing and expanding those relationships as well as identifying new areas for partnerships. This information will help the team define specific goals and objectives.

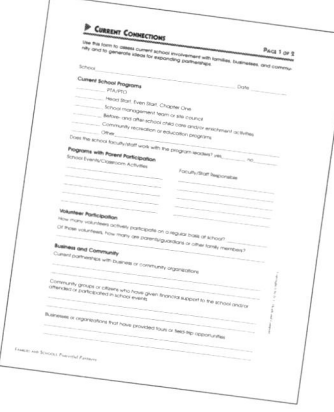

Expanding Data Collection

To deepen understanding of the current status of parent involvement throughout the school, the team can learn about the perspectives of parents, teachers, and the principal using the *Parent Participation Questionnaire* and *Perspectives on School-Home Relationships*. It is suggested that schools use the *Questionnaire* when beginning to use the *Families and Schools* model and the more detailed *Perspectives* surveys after having more experience with the model.

Parent Participation Questionnaire

Description Specific questions for parents/guardians regarding the types of involvement they want with the school and any barriers that may be preventing or limiting their participation

Function The team will use this information to guide their choice of activities and events to involve parents and families as well as to ensure that specific barriers mentioned by parents/guardians are addressed.

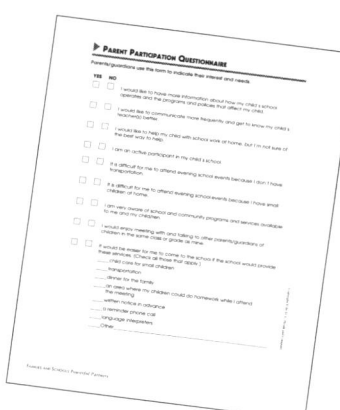

Perspectives on School-Home Relationships

Description Three parts—*Teachers' Survey, Parents' Survey,* and *Administrators' Survey*—gather in-depth information from different points of view about what is currently happening within the school to involve families; collects suggestions for improving relationships between home and school

Function Surveys are distributed to appropriate individuals, completed, and returned to the team. Survey questions can also be used to gather information through telephone interviews. The team will collate information and use it to help determine goals and objectives. The results of the completed surveys may be valid for one to three years, depending on the rate of student and faculty turnover.

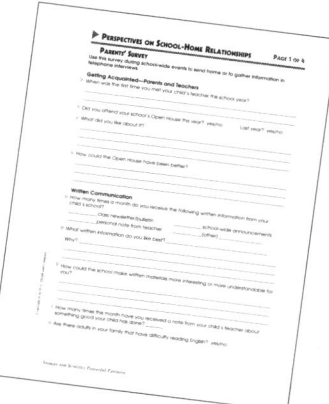

Successful strategies enhance distribution and return of questionnaires.

- Allow people to respond anonymously to encourage honesty.
- Communicate the purpose of the surveys and acknowledge people for their participation.
- Select families randomly from the school roster to ensure diverse representation.
- Provide access to all families with translation of surveys into home languages.
- Specify a date for return of surveys; make reminder phone calls if necessary. Send out two to three times as many surveys as desired be returned.
- Encourage return of surveys with incentives.

Exploring Strengths, Resources, and Opportunities for Improvement

After the team has gathered information from several sources, it can begin to define areas in which the school already excels in its parent involvement efforts and areas that need improvement. The *Summary of Survey Results* is designed to correspond to *Perspectives on School-Home Relationships* for organizing data. The *Team Planning Charts* are provided for the team's use in understanding and clarifying current and potential resources existing in classrooms, the school, and the community. This information supplements data collected on *Current Connections*.

Summary of Survey Results

Description   Information gathered in *Perspectives on School-Home Relationships* and recorded by category

Function   The survey is used to collate and organize responses to specific questions in several categories. The team should look for patterns of responses on surveys and record them on the form. Note any discrepancies between the perspectives of teachers and parents and agreement about the strengths and weaknesses.

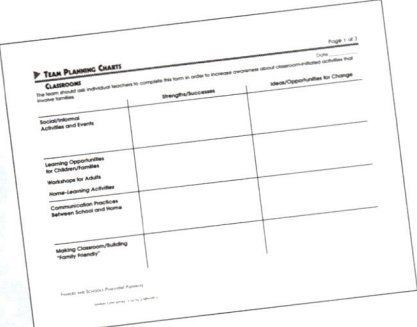

Team Planning Charts

Description   Three charts—*Classrooms, All School, Current/Potential Resources*—identify strengths in the school-home partnership, individual classrooms, and whole school efforts. Documentation of resources available from groups and individuals within the school, from students and families, from the district office, and from community groups and local businesses

Function   Charts identify and document current successful activities occurring within the school, enabling the team to build on what currently exists and draw upon the resources available within classrooms, the school, and the community. Coordinating current activities with goals and objectives for future parent involvement activities makes efficient use of time and resources and ensures success for the team.

DESIGN AND IMPLEMENTATION

Once the team has completed the *Research and Exploration* phases, it is ready to design and implement a family involvement program that responds appropriately to the needs and interests of the school's families and staff, builds on existing strengths and recognized successes, and utilizes as many resources as possible.

Determining a Focus

It has been mentioned earlier that accomplishing tangible results is crucial to ensuring ongoing commitment, motivation, and participation in team efforts. By prioritizing the many opportunities for change, the team can narrow its focus, decide what it will do in a given period of time, and succeed in achieving positive outcomes. Teams that do not define a central area of interest may become overwhelmed by the magnitude of the task of involving staff, families, and the community. Methods to focus team efforts include choosing one program goal for concentration, deciding on a reasonable number of activities in a particular theme, and limiting outreach efforts and communication improvements to one grade each year. One particularly successful way teams have narrowed their focus is by deciding on a target group of families with whom to begin outreach efforts. Each school has a unique student population, and teams should know from their research which segments of the population are not currently involved. The team can focus efforts on that population of families. By focusing on a particular segment of the population, the team can channel their efforts to a specific set of objectives. Consider the experience of one team from an urban district.

The team identified several segments of the population that faced significant barriers to participation, including non-English speaking parents/guardians, those whose children were bussed to the school from a community six miles away, and parents of children in Special Education. In setting their goals and expectations, the team decided to prioritize outreach to Spanish-speaking parents/guardians. Though they encouraged all families to participate, they focused attention on overcoming language barriers by offering concurrent workshops in Spanish, adding a Spanish translation of the newsletter, and printing all flyers on two sides—one English, the other Spanish. They sought support from bilingual staff and community members to make families feel comfortable at school events.

The team was rewarded by positive feedback from these families and by a sense of accomplishment at having involved families who had not previously participated in school events. The following year, the team determined that its focus would be families who lived outside the immediate school community and/or whose children were bussed to school. The team succeeded in reaching more of these families and maintained efforts with Spanish-speaking families as well.

Developing Goals and Objectives

After reviewing the results of surveys and exploring strengths and opportunities for change and improvement, team members should prioritize goals and set objectives using questions to create discussion.

- What can we do to remove barriers so that all families can participate?
- Where is the greatest potential for strengthening relationships with families?
- What information about the school would be most useful to parents/guardians?
- How can we enhance communication methods between school and home?
- In which areas could a small amount of effort lead to immediate, observable benefits for teachers and families?
- Which areas need long-term work?
- How can we best utilize our resources and strengths to create a variety of school-wide and classroom-initiated efforts to involve *all* families as active partners?

A balanced and comprehensive plan for family involvement should include goals and objectives from each of three categories.

Social/Informal Activities and Events

The purpose of these events is to encourage school staff and families to interact with one another on an informal, friendly basis. Activities in this category include playground or building work parties, potluck meals combined with a student performance, and opportunities to share cultural backgrounds. Specific examples from *Families and Schools* teams include a volleyball game between staff and parents, recreation night for staff, children, and families from one grade level, a Valentine's Day sweetheart dance for teachers and children and their families, and winter caroling parties.

Communication/Environment Improvements

Increasing or enhancing communication methods and making changes in the school environment itself (building and facilities) can have a powerful impact on strengthening school-home partnerships. The results of these efforts are visible and tangible and bring an immediate sense of accomplishment. It is recommended that every team has at least one goal in this category each year. Some of the options for development include homework hotlines (recorded information from the teacher for use by students and their parents), mobile telephones in each classroom, parent centers within the school, posting welcome signs in home languages of all families in the entrance hall, and posting directional signs to the office from each entrance.

Structured Learning Opportunities

Parents/guardians need information on the school's programs, curriculum, and expectations for their children. They need introductions to faculty members who have regular contact with their children and a clear understanding of the teacher's approach and philosophy. Parents need to understand all of the ways they can be involved in their children's education and in the school with specific ideas about how to work with their children at home to support the teacher's/school's efforts.

The *Families and Schools* program includes Workshops and materials for educators to use with families to develop positive school-home relationships. *Workshops for Families and Educators* is the teams' source for organizing, conducting, implementing, and evaluating events, activities, and Workshops. Activities designed to involve children and family members in learning together at home are included in each Workshop as well as described in this chapter in the section *Including Home-Learning Activities* and *Using the Families and Schools Workshops*.

Goals and objectives should be as specific as possible, including expected dates or time lines for implementation. This information should be recorded on the *Team Goals and Objectives* chart.

Team Goals and Objectives

Description A statement of the team's vision, goals, and objectives for the year

Function The team uses this form as a permanent record, to be filed with other planning documents. The team can revise their plans as necessary, but it is recommended that they fill out a new sheet and indicate the date revised. It is important to maintain this record, since the team will evaluate its progress in relation to the stated goals and objectives. It will also be beneficial to the next year's planning to look back at the prior year's plans. Planning and evaluation documents will also be useful as an orientation as new members join the team.

Examples

GOAL
To increase informal contact between school staff and families

Objective
Invite families for an ice-cream social and to visit classrooms and meet teachers prior to the first day of school.

Objective
Expand Open House to include a meal and tours of the school led by teachers and students.

GOAL

To increase parents'/guardians' awareness of what happens during the school day and how they can support their children's learning.

Objective

Facilitate *Workshop One* during the month of September.

Objective

Prepare a simple video introducing families to "a day at school" to be shown during the Workshop. (Refer to *Workshops for Families and Educators* for detailed outlines, Workshop facilitation, and video production guidelines.)

Learning from Research

National research on parent involvement and its effect on student achievement offers insights for planning and setting goals. Anne T. Henderson* has identified several roles in which parents can serve as partners in education. Parents can be involved as advocates, volunteers, learners, experts, decision makers, audience members, and "just interested people." Participation in all of these capacities helps to build bridges between school and home. Parents/guardians and teachers should be encouraged to participate in activities that make the best use of their skills and interests, suit their schedules and needs, and have the greatest benefit to their children's learning.

Some parent involvement practices are used more frequently than others. Volunteering in classrooms or for field trips comes to most people's minds when they think of parent involvement. Many schools and districts are including parents as volunteers on committees and in decision-making roles as part of restructuring efforts. Though these are valid and helpful ways to involve parents, research has demonstrated that certain forms of parent involvement are more effective in improving student achievement and success in school. The most effective forms of parent involvement are those that engage parents in working directly with their children on home-learning activities and those that develop the relationship between teachers and parents/guardians. The *Families and Schools* model is based on these understandings and incorporates the most effective forms of parental involvement in its structure, recommended activities, and Workshops.

According to research on the *Families and Schools* model, certain team actions have proved more effective than others in achieving program goals. Citizens Education Center has compiled action strategies that can dramatically increase the success of family involvement events and the team's ability to achieve objectives, specifically in the areas of invitation, content and conduct of family involvement sessions, and motivation.

The most effective strategies are listed first, followed by other strategies that are effective if used in combination.

*Anne T. Henderson, Senior Consultant, National Committee for Citizens in Education, Washington, D.C.

Strategies   **Invitation** *What Works?*

We put our emphasis on inviting parents to join us rather than notifying them of meetings they are to attend.

Personal, face-to-face invitations from the principal, teachers, counselor, or other staff such as the school secretary

Reminder phone calls from staff members

Announcements or short presentations at other parent meetings, such as kindergarten orientations, fund-raisers, or other school events

Recruitment through students: presentations in classrooms reminding students to encourage their parents to attend; small incentives for students whose parents attend; and/or prizes for the classroom with the highest parent attendance

Personalized invitations written by students

Flyers with RSVPs for preregistration, especially with personal notes added by a teacher

Strategies   **Content and Conduct** *What Works?*

When we are with parents, we spend at least as much time listening as we do telling.

Programs that incorporate a variety of activities, such as a family meal, children's performance, Home-Learning Activities, and a Workshop or brief presentation

Performances featuring children or teachers or their participation in demonstrations of school programs or resources

Opportunities for parents to interact informally with the principal, teachers, and other parents, especially if they can raise concerns that get a supportive response

Informal, interactive programs that allow time for ice-breakers, humor, socializing, small-group discussions, and question-and-answer periods

I think I'm like anyone else. I'll go to an evening meeting if someone's expecting me, if I think my time will be well spent, or if I know I'll enjoy myself.

Phone reminders the day before the event and "We missed you" calls to people who did not attend (especially if they did respond in advance)

Food, in the form of a simple, free meal or substantial snack for adults and children

Incentives, such as raffles or free items and door prizes given at the "opening bell" (Books are particularly valued.)

Specific roles for many people, combined with acknowledgment and public appreciation of those in attendance and anyone who supported the team or the event in any way

Incorporating Successful Strategies

Whatever the team's specific goals, objectives, or agenda, it is important to incorporate a variety of proven methods for success. While requiring a little extra planning, incorporating these ideas improves attendance. The team can avoid weak attendance (and disappointment) by following key strategies.

Strategies

To reach large numbers of families

- Make it a fun event.

- Schedule and advertise the event well in advance.

- Ask children to prepare invitations.

- Arrange something special for children to do; get them excited ahead of time.

- Provide a meal and arrange for transportation.

- Call and invite parents to attend.

To reach non-English speaking families

- Consult with the cultural focus group in the community and/or the ESL teacher on staff.

- Ask people to spread the word about your event.

- Call and invite parents in their home language(s).

- Provide facilitation and written information in their home language(s).

- Offer transportation.

- Involve children in the event; they can help orient their parents.

To disseminate information or ideas

- Create an appealing title.

- Include humor and fun.

- Serve a meal.

- Schedule the Workshop at a convenient time.

- Include time for warm-up and socialization.

- Provide an opportunity to discuss information in small groups.

- Make sure that information is relevant and meaningful to parents.

To establish dialogue with parents

- Provide quality child care for all ages.

- Schedule time for socializing.

- Wear casual clothes.

- Join parents in small-group discussions.

- Ask for input and opinions.

- Acknowledge and appreciate all contributions to discussion.

To increase support for parents

- Schedule several weekly sessions and encourage repeat attendance.

- Arrange for carpooling or ride sharing.

- Seat parents with others who have children in the same grade.

- Focus on topics such as discipline, conflict resolution, or stress management.

- Give parents/guardians a chance to share their questions, concerns, and suggestions.

- Provide an opportunity for parents to talk with each other informally.

Including *Home-Learning Activities*

Home-Learning Activities (HLA) create a foundation of support and commitment within families that evolves into other forms of participation in education. The following "chain model" shows how parents, as teachers of their children, can influence their children's success in school. *

▶ PARENTS AS LEARNERS AND TUTORS OF THEIR CHILDREN

CHAIN A CHILD MOTIVATION	CHAIN B CHILD SKILL	CHAIN C PARENT SELF-IMAGE

PARENT LEARNS HOW TO TEACH OWN CHILD

↓

PARENT GIVES CHILD INDIVIDUAL ATTENTION AND TEACHES NEW SKILLS

CHILD SEES THAT PARENT PERCEIVES EDUCATION AS IMPORTANT

PARENT PERCEIVES OWN NEW COMPETENCE. COMMUNICATES CONFIDENCE AND FATE CONTROL TO CHILD

CHILD LEARNS SKILLS BETTER

CHILD IS MOTIVATED TO SUCCEED IN SCHOOL

CHILD FEELS CONFIDENT HE/SHE CAN PERFORM

CHILD PERFORMS BETTER ON TESTS

* Mimi Stearns, Parent Involvement in Compensatory Education Programs, Stanford Research Institute, 1976.

The best home-learning activities reinforce skills that are taught in the class-room by connecting school learning with the home and the community. Home-learning activities help families and children learn or practice important skills and have the additional benefit of improving self-confidence and self-esteem in both children and adults. Home-learning activities should be designed to stimulate the learning process by encouraging inquiry and further exploration. They can be simple to do, take a minimum of materials, be inexpensive or free, and be fun. Home-learning activities can be developed by individual classroom teachers or by the team and can be presented in conjunction with *Workshops for Families and Educators* or as a separate activity. Teams that have successfully implemented the *Families and Schools Home-Learning Activities* offer several strategies.

Strategies

Develop a school-wide home-learning theme for the year and create a different activity each month.

Ask teachers across grades to work together to develop specific guidelines for developmentally appropriate activities.

Require completion of HLAs as part of students' homework. Request that an adult family member sign and return the HLA to school.

Secure a central location in the school to post and display HLAs as they are completed and returned to the school.

Color code completed activities to show participation of different grade levels or display in groups according to classroom to encourage teacher participation and to motivate students.

Provide simple, clear instructions—materials needed, what to do, how to do it, what skills will be used or developed.

Limit required materials to those items commonly found in the home or provide construction paper, patterns, paper clips, or other necessary supplies in reclosable plastic bags.

Provide teachers with a large envelope to collect and record participation each month. (Use attendance sheets stapled to an envelope with a column for each month that an activity will be distributed.)

Put a team member in charge of typing and copying HLAs, coordinating the collection of activities from classroom teachers, and displaying completed activities.

Refer to *Resources* in this book for *Home-Learning Activity Planning Sheet*.

Developing Winning Formats and Agendas

Over several years, teams have explored a variety of formats and agendas and collected data on their success in reaching families. Included on the following pages are outlines of team-sponsored events that were successful in reaching diverse families and involving a high percentage of the school staff. These agendas work well because they incorporate several key strategies identified in this *Guide*. Though it is expected that each team will create its own unique agendas, these examples are provided to suggest a variety of ideas and options. Some of the agendas are for informal, social events, and others establish a successful context for sharing information through the *Workshops for Families and Educators*.

Most successful event formats include a meal. Teams have experimented with a variety of options for providing simple, nutritious, and inexpensive meals for families and staff to share. To lighten the team's efforts, they have engaged school kitchen staff, parent and staff volunteers, and high school students to help with the preparation. To purchase food items, they have solicited financial support from the PTA/PTO and local citizen groups. They have asked local grocery stores and bakeries to donate food and supplies. Some teams have had food delivered and charged participants a small fee to cover costs. Whatever the approach, providing a meal is worth the effort because it guarantees greater attendance. This aspect of developing a school-home partnership has proved so significant that the *Families and Schools* teams say, "If you feed them, they will come!"

Title	FAMILY MATH NIGHT
Content Focus	Math Can Be Fun
Audience	Parents of students in grades 1–3
Convenience Factors	Children's program with math emphasis Refreshments and snacks
Format	Workshop: *Math: An Everyday Affair* Parents make a math game to take home Families play game together
Schedule	6:45 Greeting, registration, door prizes 7:00 Child care begins 7:15 Workshop begins 8:15 Families together to play game 8:30 Raffle, closing
Recruitment	Teacher invitations Notice in school newspaper PTA/PTO bulletin Door prizes, raffle

Title	HOWDY NIGHT
Content Focus	Get to Know Your School
Audience	Families of new students
Convenience Factors	Dinner provided Child care available at no cost
Format	Dinner Workshop: *Who Can Help Families to Succeed?* School tours for adults and children
Schedule	6:00 - 7:00 Dinner 7:00 - 8:00 Workshop 8:00 - 8:30 Tours of School
Recruitment	Flyers in English, Spanish, Vietnamese Phone calls to parents of new students

Title	WHY FAMILIES MAKE ALL THE DIFFERENCE!
Content Focus	Beginning of Year Relationship Building
Audience	Parents of new students Native American families and Hispanic families
Convenience Factors	Separate workshops in English and Spanish Free child care Simple meal at no cost
Format	Warm-up activities Interactive workshop, video Small-group discussions led by staff
Schedule	6:00 Macaroni and cheese, salad 6:30 Registration for Workshop and child care 6:45 Introductions and warm-up activities 7:00 Workshops start in separate room, video of The First Day of School 8:00 Small-group discussions
Recruitment	Personal invitations and phone calls Flyers in English and Spanish

Title	MULTICULTURAL FAIR
Content Focus	Diversity Awareness and Appreciation
Audience	Students and their families Entire school
Convenience Factors	Potluck supper Transportation by taxi cab (local donation)
Format	Meal together Professional dance and storytelling performance Children's performances Social event
Schedule	5:30 Children's performances 6:30 Potluck supper 7:15 Dance and storytelling 7:45 Acknowledgments, closing
Recruitment	Advertised in advance Notice on lunch menu Sign-up for potluck supper Reminder presentations in classrooms

Using the *Families and Schools* Workshops

Workshops for Families and Educators, the second source in the *Families and Schools* program, outlines the process for facilitators to organize and implement Workshops, activities, and events and describes useful group process techniques. The book also contains detailed ready-to-use plans for ten different Workshop topics to establish strong relationships between parents and teachers.

Families and Schools Workshop Goals

To develop trust and comfort levels between school personnel and parents

To inform parents with timely and relevant information about a school's programs

To develop and coordinate activities between school and home that supplement and reinforce the school curriculum

To stimulate the exchange of ideas and information between parents and teachers about what they can do together to support children's learning and success

To expand families' knowledge of their roles and responsibilities in their children's education

To help parents develop awareness of a child's development

To help parents gain awareness of and access to their school and community programs, services, and resources

The first four Workshops provide basic information parents need in order to understand the school's programs and operations; their roles and responsibilities in the education of their children; how to make the most of parent-teacher conference time; and how to work effectively with teachers. The remaining six Workshops support and expand these basic concepts, creating opportunities for families and schools to share information regarding learning objectives, positive communication, and important milestones in children's development and education. *Workshops for Families and Educators* emphasizes ideas and suggestions for working with diverse families and includes supplemental Workshop materials for duplication.

Workshops for Families and Educators is a valuable component in any school-wide plan to increase family involvement. The team will choose Workshops that are relevant to their school population and will share the responsibility for planning, organizing, implementing, and evaluating. Facilitators and presenters may be members of the team, school staff, community members, or parents/guardians. Time to conduct the Workshop activities depends on group size, audience participation and needs, and facilitator's style and preparation. As a guideline, the Workshops as outlined usually take one and one half hours to complete. By choosing among activity offerings, teams can select timely and relevant ideas and materials and incorporate them as described in the section in this Guide, *Developing Winning Formats and Agendas*.

SUMMARY

A clear vision, a structured process, and consistent action toward long-range goals are required in successful planning.

Appropriate, effective, and realistic planning occurs when the team is informed about current efforts to involve families, understands the perceptions of teachers, parents, and citizens, and has knowledge of the potential resources within the school community.

By learning from and incorporating the successful strategies identified by educational researchers and experienced teams, the team's potential for disappointment is minimized and the school's capacity to create positive outcomes is maximized.

A school can dramatically increase its ability to secure family support for *every* student by implementing a variety of approaches to parent involvement, including structured learning opportunities for parents and families, informal social gatherings, improvements to the physical school environment, and adding and enhancing communication between school and home.

DOCUMENTING PROGRESS AND RESULTS

- ▷ **PURPOSE AND METHODS**

- ▷ **DOCUMENTATION AND SUMMARIES**

- ▷ **EVALUATION AND NEXT STEPS**

PURPOSE AND METHODS

Documenting progress and evaluating results are the last two steps of the six-step process in the *Families and Schools* model and are crucial to effective program implementation and improvement. All suggestions for documentation and evaluation are intended to maximize the team's ability to self-correct and improve its outreach efforts over time. When following the procedures outlined, the team can expect specific outcomes.

- **The school and team will increase their ability to reach out and involve all families on a continual basis.**

- **The team will succeed in motivating teachers, parents, and other citizens to participate in team-sponsored activities.**

- **The school will gather support from the school board, district administrators, local businesses, and community organizations.**

By documenting and evaluating key aspects of each event and activity, the team engages in an action plan. The emphasis is on collecting information in an efficient manner and using it for practical purposes. Formative data enable the team to reflect on its performance and to adjust its efforts for greater success. Summative data enhance program accountability by deriving actual numbers and percentages of participation, support, and satisfaction.

In conjunction with each event, the team will gather data that enable the members to identify the factors in the process that work best and the circumstances that create the best results. They will determine the actions that reach the greatest number of families and targeted focus groups, and the actions that are the most successful involving school staff and community members.

Towards the end of each school year, the team members will reflect on their starting point, review goals and objectives, celebrate accomplishments, discuss results in relation to program goals, and plan next steps.

DOCUMENTATION AND SUMMARIES

Each form included in the *Guide* has been designed to contribute to the team's overall success, with multiple functions in the areas of data gathering, assessment, and planning. Teams may use only a few of the forms or methods in the first year of the program, adding tools as needed based on program expansion. Users are encouraged to modify the forms provided as necessary and appropriate to various populations and circumstances. To increase the team's efficiency and effectiveness over several years, it is recommended that team files be kept in a central location and organized for easy access. It is extremely beneficial for the team to look back over past goals and objectives, types of activities and events implemented, and indications of relative success with various strategies.

Gathering Information

Family Sign-In Sheet

Description   A record of adults who attended a Workshop or an event, names of their children, grade in school, and classroom teacher

Function   Data will be used with the *Attendance Worksheet* and the *Event Report* to determine the ratios of diversity among participants and to document levels of participation from individual classrooms.

Faculty and Staff Participation

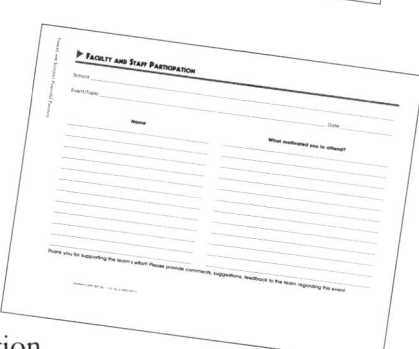

Description   Registration and response form for school staff

Function   Collected by a team member at the end of an event, these forms document the level of teacher and staff participation. Comparing information about attendance of parents and teachers can indicate the impact of teacher participation on parent participation. This form is also designed to gather feedback from teachers and staff regarding the event and what motivated them to attend. The team will use this information to improve its outreach to all staff.

Community Support Form

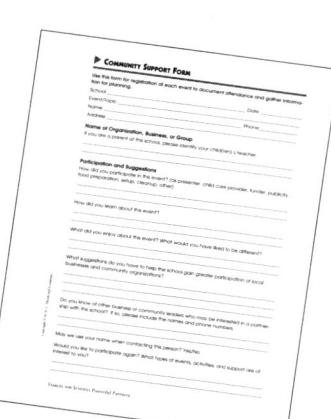

Description   Registration form for business partners, community members, student helpers, staff from other schools, and others who helped with the logistics and implementation of the event

Function   Basic data (name, address, phone) make it easy for team members to ensure that all supporters are acknowledged for their participation and contributions. This form also provides information to expand outreach to the community and to identify successful strategies for business and community involvement.

Summarizing Data

Event Report

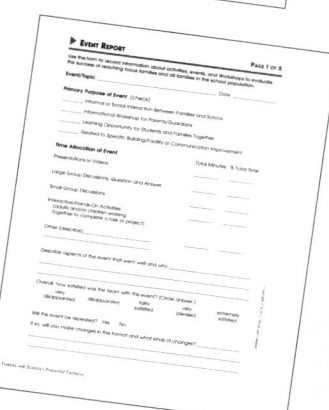

Description   Summary sheet including purpose of event, how conducted, team satisfaction, success in reaching the entire school population, and specific focus families or groups

Function   This form assists the team in assessing the success of each event and should be completed and discussed as soon as possible following the event. The coverage indexes on page 2 of the report are particularly useful for those events designed to attract parents/guardians in a particular segment of the population. A cumulative file of *Event Reports* can help determine the success of different strategies used in outreach, planning, and implementation, and can be used to improve future activities. Some information from the *Family Sign-In Sheet* and the *Annual School Profile* are used in the *Event Report*.

Attendance Worksheet

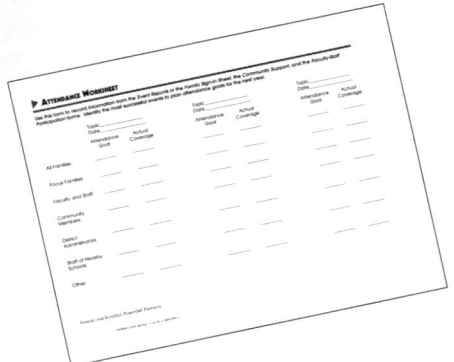

Description   Summary of attendance at several events using the *Event Report, Community Support,* and *Faculty and Staff Participation* forms

Function   This form tracks attendance for several consecutive events to provide information to the team regarding levels of participation by families, staff, and community. The team can draw conclusions regarding the types of events most successful involving these different groups and the attendance goals throughout the year.

Creating a Visual History

Teams have found that one of the most effective strategies for increasing interest in and support for their parent involvement program is the creation of visual documentation of *Families and Schools* events: photographs and video-tapes of participants and events, posters describing the event and its outcomes, signs acknowledging support from local groups and businesses, and bulletin boards displaying completed *Home-Learning Activities*. Visual documentation of team activities influences interest, motivation, and participation by students, school staff, and parents.

Visual displays build an historical memory of parent involvement efforts. They provide information to people who did not attend and delight those who see themselves participating. Displays are used in school halls, display cases, and on bulletin boards or mounted on walls. Teams keep notebooks or scrapbooks of photos, invitations, flyers, letters of support from the community, and articles from the newspaper or school bulletin. Quotes from parents and family members can inspire other parents and affirm the team's efforts. Teams also post a list of all staff members and families who attended or helped with preparation and organizations that contributed. With these visual reminders, families, educators, and community members will be more inclined to make participation a priority.

▶ EVALUATION AND NEXT STEPS

The annual evaluation process should be initiated and led by the team and may include additional staff, parent, or other community members. The evaluation is designed to generate information regarding how well the school has accomplished the program goals and to determine areas for future outreach and improvement.

Three forms are included in the *Guide* to assist the team in completing a thorough review and evaluation of their accomplishments: the *Evaluation Checklist, Key Questions,* and *Year in Review.* It is recommended that the team review documentation and planning data from significant events during the year prior to or in conjunction with completing the *Annual Evaluation Forms.*

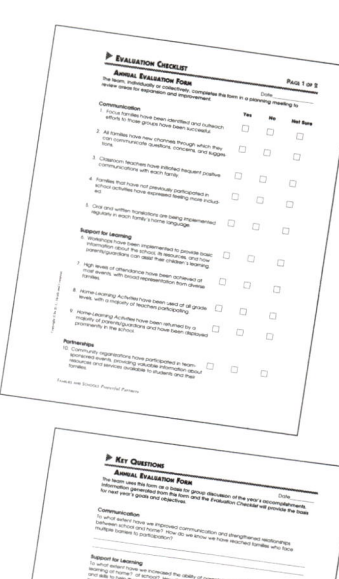

Evaluation Checklist

Description   A checklist of possible accomplishments using the *Families and Schools* model

Function   The form can be filled out by each member of the team or together in a planning meeting. The team should review responses to the statements listed on the form and note potential areas for expansion and improvement.

Key Questions

Description   Questions grouped by categories including communication, support for learning, partnerships, collaboration, and school changes

Function   Data used by the team as a basis for team discussion and assessment of their accomplishments.

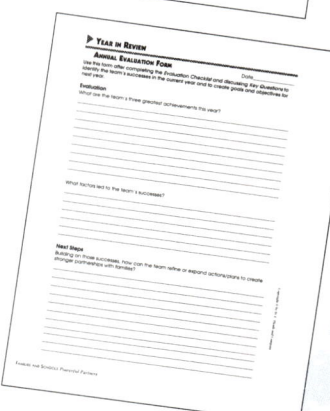

Year in Review

Description   Highlights successes and indicates plans for expanding and enhancing partnerships

Function   To be used by the team after completing the *Evaluation Checklist* and discussing *Key Questions.* Responses on this form will be used to create goals and objectives for the next school year.

The true success of *Families and Schools: Powerful Partners* teams is evident in the ability of team members to learn from their experiences and to build on small successes. Acknowledging and documenting team actions and outcomes focuses on *what works* and provides the inspiration and motivation to persist in the parent involvement effort. All positive changes in attitudes, behavior, daily operations, or school environment including minor ones should be acknowledged. It is the small, positive changes that transform the school culture over time. Once they have been identified, the team can begin to nurture and support the growth of those changes.

When the team has determined the most successful events and activities of the past year, it should consider adding one or more effective strategies described in Chapter Four to expand and enhance the next year's accomplishments. In determining future directions, one of the greatest challenges for a team is to choose from many possibilities. It is important to avoid trying to accomplish too much too soon or setting expectations too high, especially in the first year. The team should make choices based on the needs and interests of families, teachers, and team members. Select activities that generate excitement and enthusiasm among staff, families, and students and discontinue those that become a struggle or seem to consume large amounts of time or energy. If an event meets the program and team goals and is well received by staff, children, and families, do not hesitate to repeat it. Repeating successful events contributes to team visibility and program stability and conserves the team's resources. Some of the most successful activities can become annual events, gaining greater participation each year. To maintain essential energy and motivation for the partnership effort, celebrate within the team, publicize accomplishments within the school and the community, notify newspapers, acknowledge contributors, share team plans, and invite staff and community members to help plan the next year's exciting events.

Tips for Success

▶ **DO** prioritize activities that generate excitement and enthusiasm.

▶ **DO** conserve the team's planning time by making decisions in a timely manner.

▶ **DO** repeat successful events, especially if they are energizing, inspiring, or fun.

▶ **DO** take advantage of local resources.

▶ **DO** continue to add new members to the team.

▶ **DO** interact with other schools and borrow ideas from them.

▶ **DON'T** become discouraged if you don't get the results you want immediately.

▶ **DON'T** set yourselves up for failure by setting unreasonable expectations.

▶ **DON'T** try to accomplish everything all at once.

▶ **DON'T** continue activities that drain your energy or resources.

As the team moves forward with decisions and actions to create successful Workshops and events, it is important to remember the purpose of *Families and Schools: Powerful Partners*—to build relationships to support children's learning.

Ensuring success for children in today's world is an overwhelming task for any of us alone. Together we can and *do* make a difference.

SUMMARY

Documentation of progress and results is integral to effective planning, implementation, and improvement of the family involvement program. It is essential in securing resources and financial support.

Using a planned sequence of steps and information-gathering forms, the team reviews its goals, actions, and achievements and assesses results in relation to the goals. The team can then plan the next steps.

By providing visual documentation of team actions and program outcomes, the team can inspire and motivate students, families, teachers, and citizens, resulting in increased participation and commitment to school-home-community partnerships.

A school will never truly be excellent unless it involves parents.

Anne T. Henderson

National Committee for Citizens in Education

RESOURCES

- ▷ **TEAM DEVELOPMENT**

- ▷ **INITIAL ASSESSMENT**

- ▷ **DATA COLLECTION**

- ▷ **TEAM PLANNING**

- ▷ **EVENT DOCUMENTATION**

- ▷ **ANNUAL EVALUATION**

RESOURCES FOR *FAMILIES AND SCHOOLS* TEAMS

USAGE/CHAPTER	TITLE
TEAM DEVELOPMENT Chapter Two	▶ Team Members' Roles and Responsibilities ▶ Team Member List ▶ One Year Calendar of Team Activities ▶ Setting Goals and Organizing for Teamwork
INITIAL ASSESSMENT Chapter Four	▶ Annual School Profile ▶ Qualities of Effective School-Home Partnerships ▶ Current Connections

DATA COLLECTION
Chapter Four
	▶ Parent Participation Questionnaire
	▶ Perspectives on School-Home Relationships
	   • Parents' Survey
	   • Teachers' Survey
	   • Administrators' Survey
	▶ Summary of Survey Results

TEAM PLANNING
Chapter Four
	▶ Team Planning Charts
	   • Classrooms
	   • All School
	   • Current/Potential Resources
	▶ Team Goals and Objectives
	▶ HLA Planning Sheet
	▶ Three-Year Summary of a Team's Accomplishments

EVENT DOCUMENTATION Chapter Five	▶ Family Sign-In Sheet ▶ Faculty and Staff Participation ▶ Community Support Form ▶ Event Report ▶ Attendance Worksheet
ANNUAL EVALUATION Chapter Five	▶ Evaluation Checklist ▶ Key Questions ▶ Year in Review

The tools for developing school-home partnerships with the *Families and Schools* program are based on documents used successfully by teams in Washington State. In some cases, the forms have been modified for a national audience. Users are encouraged to choose the forms that facilitate the team's efforts and to modify them as necessary. All forms are reproducible.

Use this form to clarify tasks to be accomplished and to organize and assign responsibilities to team members.

Communications Coordinator
■ Notifies appropriate media about family involvement activities
■ Provides information to the faculty and staff about program goals, events, and Workshops, including agenda, location, date, and time
■ Makes informative presentations at staff meetings, community meetings, Open House, PTA/PTO meetings

NAME _____

Invitation Coordinator
■ Coordinates personal phone calls to targeted families
■ Finds translators to communicate with families in their home languages
■ Creates and displays posters announcing events for the school and community
■ Writes and makes copies of invitations to distribute in the classrooms

NAME _____

Child Care Coordinator
■ Coordinates developmentally appropriate child care for Family Nights
■ Arranges logistics and registration for child care
■ Finds adequate numbers of qualified adults to provide child care

NAME _____

Workshop Facilitator
■ Welcomes, affirms, rewards, and recognizes all families
■ Conducts the Workshops through the scheduled agenda and provides guidance for small group work
■ Takes appropriate action to address the concerns, questions, and suggestions that arise at the Workshops

NAME _____

Logistics Coordinator
■ Makes building and room arrangements for Family Night events
■ Prepares and displays locator signs inside and outside the building
■ Responds to transportation needs of families
■ Coordinates preparation of meals and/or snacks

NAME _____

FAMILIES AND SCHOOLS *Powerful Partners*

Finance and Budget Coordinator

- Assists the team in raising money to cover Workshop expenses
- Monitors income and expenses; informs team regarding finances

NAME _____

Materials Coordinator

- Buys or solicits donations, supplies, and materials for team events
- Prepares any written flyers or handouts for Workshops
- Assists data collector with sign-in and registration forms

NAME _____

Historian

- Assists with planning, narrating, and taping videos of the school setting for parent audiences
- Arranges for photographs or videos to be taken of Family Night activities
- Sets up visual wall displays in the school following each event
- Provides and posts a list of the families and staff who attend each event

NAME _____

Data Collector 1*

- Determines data collection methods to be used
- Collects *Sign-In Sheets* from registration
- Designs a plan for assigning *Home-Learning Activities*
- Writes up notes on the session

NAME _____

Data Collector 2

- Works with Data Collector 1 to gather appropriate information
- Completes *Attendance Worksheet* using *Sign-In Sheets* and *Annual School Profile*
- Reports findings to the team during the next planning session

NAME _____

*For data collection, it is recommended that the same one or two team members be responsible for the full school year. The task requires time to become familiar with the various data collection instruments and to be consistent when gathering and collating this information.

▶ TEAM MEMBER LIST

Complete at the first team meeting. Make a copy for each team member and one to file.

School Year _____

Name	Position*	Address	Phone
1.			
2.			
3.			
4.			
5.			
6.			
7.			
8.			
9.			
10.			

Team Leader _____

Data Collectors _____

*List school staff position, parent/guardian, or community representative.

FAMILIES AND SCHOOLS *Powerful Partners*

One Year Calendar Of Team

June–July

- Principal (or team leader) gains staff and community commitment to project and invites individuals to participate on the *Families and Schools* team.

August–September

- Team meets for initial training and planning session.

- Team makes presentation to school staff and develops strategies for involvement in program activities.

- Team begins to inform and involve other individuals and groups in the school who work with families.

- Team leads a process of assessing the current level of family involvement at the school using surveys.

- Team gathers baseline data and determines methods to be used in program evaluation.

- Team enlists district assistance, including funding for specific project activities such as transportation and food for "Family Night at School" events.

- Team determines specific goals and objectives and creates an action plan for family involvement activities.

Activities

October–November

- Team members communicate their plans to local businesses, social and health services, and other community organizations.
- Team coordinates and holds first family involvement event.

- With input from key parents and community members, team outlines additional plans for reaching out to families who have previously been less involved with the school.

December–March

- Team meets regularly to plan details of family involvement activities.
- Family involvement events or workshops are held approximately once per month.

- Team initiates home-learning activities in coordination with teaching staff for the purpose of helping parents understand how to participate more in their children's learning at home.

April–May

- Team continues planning and event implementation.
- School staff recognizes and celebrates family involvement efforts and acknowledges everyone who has contributed to the program's success.

- Team assesses program successes and challenges and begins program planning for the following year.

▶ SETTING GOALS AND ORGANIZING FOR TEAMWORK

Goal-Setting
- How will the team address the major goals of the program?
- What does the team plan to accomplish this year? Next year? In three years?
- How will team members use their roles to accomplish these goals?

Implementation
- Where, when, and how often will the team meet?
- Who will facilitate the team meetings? If there are co-chairs, what are their functions? Will the facilitation responsibilities be rotated?
- How and when will meeting agendas be set?

Communication
- How will team members gather responses from their constituents?
- How will team members report back to their constituents?
- How will team members communicate with each other between meetings?

Documentation
- What is the procedure for recording and summarizing meeting minutes?
- Who will be responsible for gathering and disseminating information?
- What other record keeping is needed and how will it be maintained?

Assessment
- What measures will team members use to assess their progress?
- How will the team incorporate results and feedback into future planning?

NOTES _____

_____

_____

_____

_____

_____

_____

_____

_____

_____

_____

_____

_____

Use this form to collect information needed by the team for planning and evaluation.

Date_____

School_____School Year*_____

Address_____

_____

Phone_____

Principal_____Office Staff_____

Vision or Mission Statement_____

_____

Organization and Management (District or site based?) _____

How are parents'/guardians' concerns and suggestions solicited?_____

_____

Do parents/guardians take part in decision making?_____

Names of families that have been involved in school decision-making policies

_____

Kinds of decisions in which families have been involved _____

_____

Faculty and Staff Profile

_____ certified teachers

_____ teachers new this year

_____ teachers at this school more than 10 years

Support staff available (counselor, speech therapist, nurse, head teacher, occupational therapist, bilingual or ESL teachers, family support workers)

_____

_____

Languages spoken; special skills, knowledge, experience, abilities of faculty and staff

_____

_____

*Use records for most recently completed school year.

Student Profile

_____ total enrolled _____ grades

_____ live within walking distance

_____ bussed more than three miles

_____ attend child care before and/or after school

_____ perfect attendance

_____ given special recognition last year

What was recognition for? Where and how did acknowledgment occur? _____

_____

_____ identified as focus of concern

_____ referred to the principal

_____ retained or suspended

Student Programs

Special support programs available (Head Start, Chapter 1, ESL, resource room, before- and after-school child care, enrichment or special education, tutoring, homework classes, Extended Day Kindergarten)_____

_____

Family Profile

_____ total number of families _____ two parent/guardian families

_____ single parent families _____ mothers _____ fathers

_____ students living with someone other than parents/guardians

_____ low income (qualify for free or reduced lunch)

_____ without own transportation

_____ live more than three miles from the school

_____ speak a home language other than English

Languages represented_____

Ethnic diversity _____ African American _____ Caucasian _____ Latino/Chicano _____
Native American _____ Asian or Pacific Islander _____ Other _____

Special skills, talents, experiences in job/profession/avocation; contacts with business and community_____

▶ QUALITIES OF EFFECTIVE SCHOOL-HOME PARTNERSHIPS*

Team members complete this form prior to goal setting and discuss their responses. It may also be used as a quick survey of parent opinions at the beginning and/or end of the year.

	Rarely	Frequently	Always
Every aspect of the school climate is open, helpful, and friendly.	_____	_____	_____
Communications with parents/guardians—whether about school policies and programs or about their own children—are frequent, clear, and two-way.	_____	_____	_____
Parents are treated as collaborators in the educational process, with a strong role to play in their children's school learning and behavior.	_____	_____	_____
Parents are encouraged, both formally and informally, to comment on school policies and to share in decision making on some issues.	_____	_____	_____
The school recognizes its responsibility to build a partnership with all families. This includes parents who work outside the home, low-income families, single-parent families, families outside the immediate school area, families of color, and those whose home language is not English.	_____	_____	_____
The principal and other school administrators actively express and promote the philosophy of partnership with all families.	_____	_____	_____
The school encourages volunteer participation from parents/guardians, businesses, and the community at large.	_____	_____	_____

*Adapted from Henderson, Marburger, and Ooms, *Beyond the Bake Sale: An Educator's Guide to Working with Parents.* National Committee for Citizens in Education, 1986.

Use this form to assess current school involvement with families, businesses, and community and to generate ideas for expanding partnerships.

School_____ Date _____

Current School Programs

_____ PTA/PTO

_____ Head Start, Even Start, Chapter One

_____ School management team or site council

_____ Before- and after-school child care and/or enrichment activities

_____ Community recreation or education programs

_____ Other_____

Does the school faculty/staff work with the program leaders? yes_____ no_____

Programs with Parent Participation

School Events/Classroom Activities   Faculty/Staff Responsible

_____   _____

_____   _____

_____   _____

_____   _____

_____   _____

Volunteer Participation

How many volunteers actively participate on a regular basis at school? _____

Of those volunteers, how many are parents/guardians or other family members?

_____

Business and Community

Current partnerships with business or community organizations

_____

_____

Community groups or citizens who have given financial support to the school and/or attended or participated in school events

_____

_____

Businesses or organizations that have provided tours or field-trip opportunities

_____

_____

Expanding Current Connections

Name of Current Connection

_____

_____

Ideas for Expansion/Enhancement

_____

_____

_____

_____

Whom to Contact/How/When

_____

_____

_____

_____

_____

New Partnerships

List five to ten businesses and community organizations within the area surrounding your school.

_____

_____

_____

_____

Ideas for creating new partnerships

_____

_____

_____

_____

_____

_____

_____

_____

▶ PARENT PARTICIPATION QUESTIONNAIRE

Parents/guardians use this form to indicate their interest and needs.

YES **NO**

☐ ☐ I would like to have more information about how my child's school operates and the programs and policies that affect my child.

☐ ☐ I would like to communicate more frequently and get to know my child's teacher(s) better.

☐ ☐ I would like to help my child with school work at home, but I'm not sure of the best way to help.

☐ ☐ I am an active participant in my child's school.

☐ ☐ It is difficult for me to attend evening school events because I don't have transportation.

☐ ☐ It is difficult for me to attend evening school events because I have small children at home.

☐ ☐ I am very aware of school and community programs and services available to me and my child/ren.

☐ ☐ I would enjoy meeting with and talking to other parents/guardians of children in the same class or grade as mine.

☐ ☐ It would be easier for me to come to the school if the school would provide these services. (Check all those that apply.)

_____child care for small children

_____transportation

_____dinner for the family

_____an area where my children could do homework while I attend the meeting

_____written notice in advance

_____a reminder phone call

_____language interpreters

_____Other_____

PARENTS' SURVEY

Use this survey during school-wide events to send home or to gather information in telephone interviews.

Getting Acquainted—Parents and Teachers

► When was the first time you met your child's teacher this school year?

_____

_____

► Did you attend your school's Open House this year? yes/no   Last year? yes/no

► What did you like about it?

_____

_____

_____

► How could the Open House have been better?

_____

_____

_____

Written Communication

► How many times a month do you receive the following written information from your child's school?

_____class newsletter/bulletin   _____school-wide announcements

_____personal note from teacher   _____(other) _____

► What written information do you like best?_____

Why? _____

_____

_____

► How could the school make written materials more interesting or more understandable for you?

_____

_____

_____

► How many times this month have you received a note from your child's teacher about something good your child has done? _____

► Are there adults in your family that have difficulty reading English? yes/no

PARENTS' SURVEY

Telephone Communication

▶ How many times has your child's teacher called you on the telephone this school year? _____ For what reason(s)? _____

_____

_____

▶ Did the teacher call you at home or at work? _____   Was this convenient? yes/no

▶ Have you called your child's teacher this school year? yes/no   How many times? _____

▶ Did you call the teacher at home or at school? _____

Describe how you felt about the call._____

_____

_____

▶ If you have a question or concern about any of these situations, whom would you contact at your school? If not sure, please check **Not Sure**.

Not Sure   **Person to Contact**

_____ Your child is having difficulty with schoolwork.   _____

_____ You don't understand a school rule or policy.   _____

_____ Your child is having problems getting along with others._____

_____ You think your child is falling behind in school.   _____

_____ Your child doesn't want to go to school.   _____

_____ Your child tells you the teacher said something that you don't like.

                                                                 _____

▶ During this school year, have you talked to the people you wanted to? yes/no

Parent-Teacher Conferences

▶ Did you or another person in your family attend a Parent-Teacher Conference for your child this fall? yes/no

▶ What did you like about the conference?_____

_____

▶ What could have improved the conference?_____

_____

▶ Did you get to know your child's teacher better? yes/no
▶ Do you think the teacher got to know you better? yes/no

How could you tell?_____

_____

PARENTS' SURVEY

Home Visits

► Has your child's teacher visited you in your home this school year? yes/no If so, what was it like?

_____

_____

► How would you feel if your child's teacher came to your home to meet you and to talk about how you could work together to help your child succeed in school?

_____

_____

Volunteering/Sharing Cultural Heritage

► Have you been asked to volunteer at your child's school?   yes/no
   If so, who asked you? _____

_____

► If you volunteer to help the class or school, how many hours each month do you volunteer? _____   What kinds of things do you do? _____

_____

_____

_____

► If you do not volunteer at this time, would you be interested in talking with someone at the school about ways to partipate? yes/no What kinds of things would you like to do?

_____

_____

_____

► Have you ever shared aspects of your cultural heritage with staff or students at this school? yes/no   If not, would you like to?

_____

_____

_____

Homework and *Home-Learning Activities*

► How many times a week does your child have homework? _____

► Does homework cause problems in your home? Explain._____

_____

_____

PARENTS' SURVEY

► How often do you help your child with homework? _____

► Where in your house does your child generally do his/her homework?_____

_____

► What else do you do at home to help your child learn (read stories, play games, cook, other)?

_____

_____

► Would you like more ideas for ways you can help your child learn at home?

_____

► What kinds of ideas or help would you like?

_____

_____

Relationships/Working with Interpreters and Cultural Specialists

► Does your child's teacher think you are a good parent? yes/no   How do you know?

_____

_____

► How would you describe your relationship with your child's teacher this year?

_____

_____

► What could make it better?

_____

_____

► The most important quality in a teacher is_____

► The most important quality in a principal is _____

► Would you find it helpful to work with an interpreter or a cultural specialist? yes/no

Secretaries, Bus Drivers, Custodians, and Food Service Staff

► Which people who work for the school have made you feel welcome and comfortable?

_____

_____

► Have you ever felt judged or criticized by anyone in the school? Please explain.

_____

_____

TEACHERS' SURVEY

Use this form to gather information about each teacher's level of involvement and challenges in building partnerships with parents/guardians.

Getting Acquainted—Parents and Teachers

▶ Did you have contact with any parents/guardians before school in the fall?   yes/no
If so, please describe.

_____

_____

_____

▶ What percentage of the time do you meet parents for the first time?

■ before school starts _____

■ the first week of school _____

■ at Open House _____

■ at Parent-Teacher Conferences _____

▶ What did you like about this year's (or last year's) Open House?

_____

_____

Open House would be better if _____

_____

Written Communication

▶ How many times a month do you send home the following types of written information to parents/guardians?

_____ class newsletter/bulletin   _____ all school announcements

_____ individualized notes to parents   _____ (other) _____

▶ If you send home individual notes to parents/guardians, what percent—

give positive feedback?_____   address problems/concerns?_____

▶ How many of your students have parents who are non-readers and speak English as their primary language? _____

How many of your students have ESL parents? _____

Are there resources for written translation available? yes/no   How are these used?

_____

_____

_____

_____

TEACHERS' SURVEY

Telephone Communication

How many parents do you contact on the telephone each month? _____

► Of these calls, what percent—

are positive? _____   are problems/concerns? _____

How could calling parents/guardians be made easier ?_____

How many parents/guardians call you each month? _____

Do parents call you at school or at home? _____

► When parents/guardians have questions/concerns about their children, what percent of the time do they—

- call you on the phone (at home or at school)? _____
- drop by the school to talk to you? _____
- make an appointment to see you? _____
- send a note with the child? _____

Which method(s) do you prefer?_____

Parent-Teacher Conferences

► What percent of the students had at least one parent/guardian come to the Parent-Teacher Conferences in the fall?_____

Generally, who is included in the conference?_____
_____
_____

► How do you deal with parents who are reluctant to come to the school for conferences or do not come as scheduled?
_____
_____
_____

► Do you send home notices to parents/guardians about the conferences *before* the conference?   yes/no   If so, please describe._____
_____
_____
_____

What percent of the time to you talk/share information in the conference?_____

What percent of the time does the parent/guardian talk/ask questions? _____

TEACHERS' SURVEY

Home Visits

▶ Have you made home visits to your students' families this year? yes/no

For what purpose(s)? _____

Were the visits effective in meeting your goals? yes/no/somewhat Explain_____

_____

_____

Volunteering/Sharing Cultural Heritage

▶ Do any parents/guardians volunteer in your classroom? yes/no
How many?_____

How many hours per month do volunteers help you? _____

What types of things do they do?

_____

_____

How did you arrange for these volunteers?

_____

_____

▶ If you have parents/guardians doing volunteer work for you outside the classroom and/or after school hours, please describe.

_____

_____

▶ How have families shared their cultural heritage in your classroom? Please describe.

_____

_____

Homework and *Home-Learning Activities*

What percent of the parents/guardians assist their children with homework?_____

1 Most of my parents **2** Some of my parents **3** Few of my parents

____ provide a space for work

____ structure the time (before dinner or TV after school)

____ do the assignment for the child

____ correct the assignment

____ reward/punish the child

TEACHERS' SURVEY

▷ What percent of the parents/guardians do learning activities at home (other than home-work) with children at least two times a week? _____

▷ Where do they find their ideas? (school newsletters and activities, magazines, children's suggestions, parents' ideas, teachers' ideas)

_____
_____
_____
_____

▷ How do you encourage parents who are non-readers or ESL parents to help their children?

_____
_____
_____
_____

Relationships/Working with Interpreters and Cultural Specialists

▷ What strategies do you use to communicate with the families in your classroom? (single parents, different educational levels, diverse cultures) _____

_____
_____

Please share a strategy you have used successfully.

_____
_____
_____
_____

▷ How many cultures are represented by the students' families? _____

▷ Are interpreters or cultural specialists available to assist you in working with families? yes/no

▷ What would help you to work more effectively with these families?

_____
_____

▷ Would you like more opportunities to exchange ideas with other districts for working with diverse families?

_____
_____

ADMINISTRATOR'S SURVEY

Use this form to gather information about the principal's perspective and the current status of parent involvement in the school.

Philosophy/Procedures

► What is the school's philosophy/goals for building school-home relationships?

_____

_____

_____

► What types of policies are in place regarding school-home contact? (type, frequency, restrictions)

_____

_____

_____

_____

_____

Communication

► Is there an expectation that the faculty/staff will meet these expectations?

YES   NO

☐   ☐   Send written communications including personal notes.

☐   ☐   Telephone families with positive feedback/for problem solving

☐   ☐   Use the phone after school hours

☐   ☐   Make home visits (for specific circumstances?)

☐   ☐   Utilize volunteers

Outside Resources

► Are staff members encouraged to use cultural specialists to build relationships with culturally diverse families? Yes/No

What resources are available from the district central office to assist staff?

_____

_____

_____

_____

ADMINISTRATOR'S SURVEY

Faculty and Staff

▷ Are faculty and staff (teachers, secretaries, bus drivers, custodians, food service employees) evaluated on school-home communication? Yes/No   On what aspects?

_____

_____

▷ Which teachers have the strongest skills in building relationships with families in your school? _____

_____

_____

▷ What strategies are they currently implementing?

_____

_____

▷ With what types of families has it been particularly challenging for your staff to establish relationships?

_____

_____

_____

▷ What kinds of staff development opportunities are available to assist teachers in working effectively with these families?

_____

_____

Collaboration and Support

▷ Does the school environment support and encourage collaboration among staff members? Yes/No How?

_____

_____

▷ Do staff members openly share their strengths/needs? yes/no

▷ Are staff members comfortable asking for help from each other? yes/no How do they get help?

_____

_____

▷ What types of support do you provide staff for dealing with difficult situations that arise with parents/families?

_____

_____

▶ SUMMARY OF SURVEY RESULTS

Use this form to gather and record information from *Perspectives on School-Home Relationships.*

Category (from the survey)

_____

_____

_____

_____

_____

Strengths

_____

_____

_____

_____

_____

Areas Needing Improvement

_____

_____

_____

_____

_____

Ideas for Change

_____

_____

_____

_____

Potential Resources

_____

_____

_____

_____

CLASSROOMS

Date _____

The team should ask individual teachers to complete this form in order to increase awareness about classroom-initiated activities that involve families.

	Strengths/Successes	Ideas/Opportunities for Change
Social/Informal Activities and Events		
Learning Opportunities for Children/Families Workshops for Adults *Home-Learning Activities*		
Communication Practices Between School and Home		
Making Classroom/Building "Family Friendly"		

FAMILIES AND SCHOOLS *Powerful Partners*

▶ TEAM PLANNING CHARTS

ALL SCHOOL

Date _____

Use this form to examine the kinds of family-involvement activities that occurred during the past year.

	Strengths/Successes	Ideas/Opportunities for Change
Social/Informal Activities and Events		
Learning Opportunities for Children/Families Workshops for Adults *Home-Learning Activities*		
Communication Practices Between School and Home		
Making Classroom/Building "Family Friendly"		

▶ TEAM PLANNING CHARTS

CURRENT/POTENTIAL RESOURCES

Use this form to record ideas generated during a team brainstorming session.

Date_____

	Knowledge/ Skills	Technology	Donations/ Financial Support	Time
Individuals/ Groups in the School				
Students/ Families				
School/District Administrators				
Community Groups				
Local Businesses				

FAMILIES AND SCHOOLS *Powerful Partners*

▲ TEAM GOALS AND OBJECTIVES

Team Name _____ Date _____

Vision Statement _____

_____

▲ Goal _____

_____

	Person responsible	Target date
Objective _____	_____	_____
Objective _____	_____	_____
Objective _____	_____	_____

▲ Goal _____

_____

	Person responsible	Target date
Objective _____	_____	_____
Objective _____	_____	_____
Objective _____	_____	_____

▶ HOME-LEARNING ACTIVITY PLANNING SHEET

Use this form to plan *Home-Learning Activities.* Have families complete and return the form with the activities to school.

Topic _____

_____

_____

Skills to be used or developed

_____

_____

_____

_____

_____

_____

Materials needed

_____

_____

_____

_____

_____

_____

What to do and how to do it

_____

_____

_____

_____

_____

_____

The following family member(s) worked with_____to complete
this *Home-Learning Activity.*   (Child's first name)

_____

_____

Parent/Guardian Signature_____

Date_____

▶ FAMILIES AND SCHOOLS: POWERFUL PARTNERS

THREE-YEAR SUMMARY OF A TEAM'S ACCOMPLISHMENTS

This three-year summary of the actual experiences of successful teams in Washington State demonstrates the accomplishments possible using the *Families and Schools: Powerful Partners* model. The specific accomplishments are defined as four key areas of the team's efforts. These ideas are suggestions for realistic planning but are not intended to be all inclusive or prescriptive. Each year the team will set goals and objectives to reach out to staff, families, and the community. They will accomplish various objectives and achieve unique results and outcomes. The exact sequence of activities for each team will vary, with some events and activities repeated each year, some eliminated as a result of team evaluation process, and some revised, expanded, and strengthened in each subsequent year.

YEAR ONE

TEAM DEVELOPMENT

- Six individuals agreed to serve on the team.
- Team planning meetings held monthly before the start of the school day.
- Team name chosen and used in all communications.
- Roles and responsibilities for team members are clearly established.

OUTREACH EFFORTS

- Team gathers information about outreach efforts already in place and determines current levels of parent involvement.
- Short version of parent involvement surveys used to gain input from parents regarding their satisfaction and comfort with the school, any obstacles that may prevent their participation, and types of information that would be helpful to them in assisting their children's learning.
- Focus families in each grade level called by teachers and invited to attend Workshop.
- A local business and a community organization contacted and invited to participate in the school's efforts to involve families.
- Conferences scheduled according to family needs; child care and transportation offered.

TEAM AND STAFF ACCOMPLISHMENTS

- Team prioritizes efforts to involve families whose children face challenges to success in school.
- Team members and staff volunteers create a video to share with parents and the community, documenting a typical day at school from a child's perspective.
- Two school events are planned for families, with an emphasis on social interaction between parents and all school staff.
- Two informational sessions are conducted on areas of particular interest to parents, beginning with selected *Workshops for Families and Educators.*

DOCUMENTED RESULTS

- Attendance at first Workshop (including video showing) is more than 100 families, including 60 percent of focus families, three of whom have never come to the school before.
- 95 percent of parents/guardians attend parent conferences.
- Each student is represented by family participation in at least one school event.
- Teachers report increased communication with families of students who face challenges to school success.
- Local business owner agrees to participate as a member of the team.
- Several parents contact the principal to say how pleased they are at the increased contact with families.

FAMILIES AND SCHOOLS *Powerful Partners*

YEAR TWO

TEAM DEVELOPMENT

- One community member and one bilingual parent are added as members of the team.

- Team meetings are held once per month accompanied by potluck dinner.

- 1/2 day training is arranged to enhance knowledge and skills of team members and all staff, enabling them to reach out to all families more effectively.

- Active parent from Year One team becomes team leader.

OUTREACH EFFORTS

- In-depth surveys are used for the perspectives and opinions of parents, teachers, and administrators about several aspects of school-home partnership.

- Bilingual staff and community members serve as translators to interpret surveys for Spanish-speaking parents.

- Video created in Year One is modified to provide a version narrated in Spanish.

- Mid-year raffle is held for staff members who participated in team-sponsored parent involvement events. Second raffle is scheduled for end of year.

- Team members approach PTA/PTO president to propose a collaborative event to provide information to parents on community-sponsored activities available for children and families during the summer months.

TEAM AND STAFF ACCOMPLISHMENTS

- Opportunity to welcome students and families is created on an afternoon prior to the start of school. Snacks and guided building tours are offered, as well as a chance to meet and talk with students' classroom teachers.

- School-wide theme established each semester to promote parent participation in learning activities at home. Teachers at each grade level develop Home-Learning Activities related to the theme.

- Positive comments are communicated about each child's school experience via postcards sent to every family in the primary grades twice during the school year.

- Teachers from neighboring schools are invited to participate in or observe school-home partnership events.

- Team sponsors three evening events emphasizing the school's reading, math, and science programs and suggesting ways family members can support their children's learning at home.

DOCUMENTED RESULTS

- A permanent bulletin board is designated for school-home partnership activities and events.

- Completed home-learning activities are displayed in a main hall and continually added to throughout the year.

- Local newspaper features an article on the school's parent and community involvement successes.

- Evaluation reveals that 90 percent of families completed and returned home-learning activities and that 40 percent more Spanish-speaking families have participated in school events this year as compared to last year. Parents who live outside the immediate neighborhood (approximately 25 percent) are still underrepresented at evening events. (Only 8 percent of those attending were from outside the area.)

YEAR THREE

TEAM DEVELOPMENT

- Team joins a national parent involvement organization and receives a regular newsletter about parent involvement strategies working in schools across the country. The newsletter is made available to each teacher and items are discussed at staff meetings.

- Three team members are replaced by new, enthusiastic teacher and parent volunteers. A staff member of a local social service organization agrees to be on the team. The team of nine members now adequately represents the population diversity of the school community.

- New team members are provided with documentation of the team's activities over the past two years and given an opportunity to choose their roles and responsibilities.

- One-day team training is attended by several staff members and teacher and parent representatives from the neighboring elementary school and middle school.

OUTREACH EFFORTS

- All kindergarten and first grade teachers agree to contact families to arrange home visits prior to or during the first month of school.

- Team decides to hold an event at a community center in the neighborhood of several families who still have not attended Family Nights at school.

- Parent organized and operated carpool is set up prior to parent conferences. A few teachers decide to hold Saturday conferences for working families with scheduling difficulties.

- A partnership is formed with the privately operated on-site before and after school child care center. Center staff provides child care during Workshops. The school staff participates in a fund-raiser to benefit the child care center.

TEAM AND STAFF ACCOMPLISHMENTS

- Two new informational workshops are created based on the interests expressed by families and educators.

- Business partner is asked (and agrees) to provide $500 to purchase food for family meals prior to Workshops.

- The school newsletter features a regular column on home-learning activities parents and children can work on together at home.

- The team's most successful activities are annual events.

- The school district installs homework information "hot lines" to enhance school-home communication.

- The principal, with support from the team and the staff, writes a grant to fund creation of a parent center in an area near the main office.

DOCUMENTED RESULTS

- More than 500 calls are made to the homework "hot line" within the first week of operation.

- 100 percent of students are represented by one or more family members at fall conferences.

- The school district administration puts parent involvement training for all staff into the budget and decides to support expansion of Families and Schools: Powerful Partners in three more schools the following year.

- A local television station features the school and highlights its outreach to families and the community. The school receives inquiries from four districts regarding methods used to increase parent involvement.

- The school board acknowledges school successes using the Families and Schools model: significant increases in positive communications between school and home, a 150 percent increase in volunteers for tutoring, and dramatically reduced absenteeism and disciplinary referrals over a three-year period.

▶ FAMILY SIGN-IN SHEET

School _____   Date _____

Event/Workshop Topic _____

Your Name	**Children Enrolled in This School** (Child's first and last name/Teacher's name/Grade)

▲ Faculty and Staff Participation

School _____ Date _____

Event/Topic _____

Name	What motivated you to attend?

Thank you for supporting the team's effort! Please provide comments, suggestions, feedback to the team regarding this event.

▶ COMMUNITY SUPPORT FORM

Use this form for registration at each event to document attendance and gather information for planning.

School _____ Date _____

Event/Topic _____

Name _____ Phone_____

Address _____

Name of Organization, Business, or Group

If you are a parent at this school, please identify your child(ren)'s teacher.

_____

_____

Participation and Suggestions

How did you participate in this event? (as presenter, child care provider, funder, publicity, food preparation, setup, cleanup, other)

_____

_____

How did you learn about this event?

_____

_____

What did you enjoy about this event? What would you have liked to be different?

_____

_____

What suggestions do you have to help the school gain greater participation of local businesses and community organizations?

_____

_____

_____

Do you know of other business or community leaders who may be interested in a partnership with the school? If so, please include the names and phone numbers.

_____

_____

May we use your name when contacting this person? Yes/No

Would you like to participate again? What types of events, activities, and support are of interest to you?

_____

_____

FAMILIES AND SCHOOLS *Powerful Partners*

Use this form to record information about activities, events, and Workshops to evaluate the success of reaching focus families and all families in the school population.

Event/Topic _____ Date _____

Primary Purpose of Event (check)

_____ Informal or Social Interaction Between Families and School

_____ Informational Workshop for Parents/Guardians

_____ Learning Opportunity for Students and Families Together

_____ Related to Specific Building/Facility or Communication Improvement

Time Allocation at Event	Total Minutes	% Total Time
Presentations or Videos	_____	_____
Large Group Discussions, Question and Answer	_____	_____
Small Group Discussions	_____	_____
Interactive/Hands-On Activities (adults and/or children working together to complete a task or project)	_____	_____
Other (describe)_____	_____	_____

_____

Describe aspects of the event that went well and why._____

_____

_____

Overall, how satisfied was the team with this event? (Circle answer.)

| very disappointed | disappointed | fairly satisfied | very pleased | extremely satisfied |

Will this event be repeated?   Yes   No

If so, will you make changes in the format and what kinds of changes?._____

_____

_____

Topic _____ Date _____

Focus Families

Who were you trying to reach? (Use the list that follows to write the description.)

Focus families description _____

_____

- Families new to the school
- Male parents/family members
- Parents of color
- Low income families
- Special needs populations
- ESL Families
- Parents of Kindergartners
- Other (define) _____

Complete the coverage index to receive information about participation of any groups. Following is an example to calculate the coverage index.

Sample

a. (Describe focus families) _____families new to the school_____

b. *Number* of focus families attending: _____8_____

c. Total number of *focus families* in the school: _____22_____

d. Coverage index *(b÷c)* is percent of focus families reached ___36%___

Coverage Index

a. (Describe focus families)_____

b. Number of focus families attending:_____

c. Total number of focus families in the school: _____

d. Coverage index (b÷c) is percent of focus families reached:_____

If your event was designed to reach more than one group of parents, repeat the process.

▶ ATTENDANCE WORKSHEET

Use this form to record information from the *Event Reports* or the *Family Sign-In Sheet*, the *Community Support*, and the *Faculty-Staff Participation* forms. Identify the most successful events to plan attendance goals for the next year.

Topic _____ Date _____

Topic _____ Date _____

Topic _____ Date _____

	Attendance Goal	Actual Coverage	Attendance Goal	Actual Coverage	Attendance Goal	Actual Coverage
All Families	_____	_____	_____	_____	_____	_____
Focus Families	_____	_____	_____	_____	_____	_____
Faculty and Staff	_____	_____	_____	_____	_____	_____
Community Members	_____	_____	_____	_____	_____	_____
District Administrators	_____	_____	_____	_____	_____	_____
Staff of Nearby Schools	_____	_____	_____	_____	_____	_____
Other	_____	_____	_____	_____	_____	_____

FAMILIES AND SCHOOLS *Powerful Partners*

ANNUAL EVALUATION FORM   Date_____

The team, individually or collectively, completes this form in a planning meeting to review areas for expansion and improvement.

	Yes	No	Not Sure
Communication			
1. Focus families have been identified and outreach efforts to those groups have been successful.	☐	☐	☐
2. All families have new channels through which they can communicate questions, concerns, and suggestions.	☐	☐	☐
3. Classroom teachers have initiated frequent positive communications with each family.	☐	☐	☐
4. Families that have not previously participated in school activities have expressed feeling more included.	☐	☐	☐
5. Oral and written translations are being implemented regularly in each family's home language.	☐	☐	☐
Support for Learning			
6. Workshops have been implemented to provide basic information about the school, its resources, and how parents/guardians can assist their children's learning.	☐	☐	☐
7. High levels of attendance have been achieved at most events, with broad representation from diverse families.	☐	☐	☐
8. *Home-Learning Activities* have been used at all grade levels, with a majority of teachers participating.	☐	☐	☐
9. *Home-Learning Activities* have been returned by a majority of parents/guardians and have been displayed prominently in the school.	☐	☐	☐
Partnerships			
10. Community organizations have participated in team-sponsored events, providing valuable information about resources and services available to students and their families.	☐	☐	☐

	Yes	No	Not Sure
11. Local businesses and community agencies have been informed of school outreach activities, invited to participate, and have attended team-sponsored events.	☐	☐	☐
12. Community organizations and businesses have contributed to successful program implementation by providing publicity, materials, money, and time.	☐	☐	☐
13. At least one community member participates actively as a member of the team, and at least one new partnership has been established between the school and a local business or organization.	☐	☐	☐

Collaboration

	Yes	No	Not Sure
14. The team meets at least once per month and includes diverse parent and staff representation.	☐	☐	☐
15. The team regularly communicates progress to all staff and requests feedback from teachers and families.	☐	☐	☐
16. A majority of teachers have initiated parent involvement efforts in their classrooms and have increased positive communications with each family.	☐	☐	☐
17. A majority of the teachers have participated in planning, implementing, and evaluating the team's activities and attended at least two events.	☐	☐	☐

School Changes

	Yes	No	Not Sure
18. More emphasis is being placed on including parents as advocates, learners, experts, volunteers, decision-makers, and audience.	☐	☐	☐
19. The building has signs to welcome family and community members to the school and signs to the office and restrooms. Signs are in all home languages as well as in English.	☐	☐	☐
20 Respect for parents as educational partners is more frequently expressed throughout the school.	☐	☐	☐

ANNUAL EVALUATION FORM

Date_____

The team uses this form as a basis for group discussion of the year's accomplishments. Information generated from this form and the *Evaluation Checklist* will provide the basis for next year's goals and objectives.

Communication

To what extent have we improved communication and strengthened relationships between school and home? How do we know we have reached families who face multiple barriers to participation?

_____

_____

Support for Learning

To what extent have we increased the ability of parents/guardians to assist their children's learning at home? at school? How do we know that parents have additional knowledge and skills to help their children? What types of knowledge and skills have been increased? In what ways have we improved access to school and community resources?

_____

_____

Partnerships

To what extent have we expanded partnerships with businesses, social and health service agencies, and concerned citizens? In what ways have these partnerships increased involvement of families or directly benefited students' school success?

_____

_____

Collaboration

How successful has the team been in providing leadership and diverse representation for the family involvement effort? In what ways have faculty and staff members been active participants in planning, implementing, and evaluating team-sponsored activities? What activities have staff members initiated on their own?

_____

_____

School Changes

What changes have occurred throughout the school (policies, programs, facilities) to indicate that parents/guardians are increasingly welcomed as valued partners in the education of their children? What evidence indicates that trust and respect have grown between parents and teachers?

_____

_____

ANNUAL EVALUATION FORM

Date_____

Use this form after completing the *Evaluation Checklist* and discussing *Key Questions* to identify the team's successes in the current year and to create goals and objectives for next year.

Evaluation

What are the team's three greatest achievements this year?

_____

_____

_____

_____

_____

_____

_____

_____

_____

What factors led to the team's successes?

_____

_____

_____

_____

_____

_____

Next Steps

Building on those successes, how can the team refine or expand actions/plans to create stronger partnerships with families?

_____

_____

_____

_____

_____

_____

_____

_____

_____

_____

_____